Mountain Biking the High Sierra
Guide 3A

LAKE TAHOE – SOUTH
Eldorado, Toiyabe and Tahoe National Forests

Third Edition

by Carol Bonser & R. W. Miskimins

FINE EDGE
Productions
BISHOP, CALIFORNIA

Acknowledgments

Carol Bonser wishes to thank the following people for their help and support throughout the creation of this guidebook and the additional updates. First, my parents, for moving our family to this area years ago so we could grow up appreciating the National Forests and what they have to offer; next, my brother, Gordon, who introduced me to mountain biking and successfully kept my bike functioning for the 2,000+ miles ridden in preparing this book. I would also like to thank a group of special friends I call the "Sunday Riders," including Mike, Susan, Bob, Zeth, Diana and especially our "sweep rider," Dana, for the days spent out on the trails testing the rides so others could enjoy them in the future.

R.W. (Ray) Miskimins wishes to thank his family for their constant support and assistance through this and many other projects over the years. My wife, Bette, has been extremely helpful for this South Lake Tahoe guidebook by providing the bulk of the new photographs and many hours of critical proofreading.

Also deserving of acknowledgment are several employees of the U.S. Forest Service and numerous individuals, who in one form or another, helped in the original production or subsequent revisions of this guidebook by proof reading, answering questions, going on rides, and providing maps. And last, thanks must go to Don and Réanne Douglass for creating the series of guidebooks of which this is a part—their support and encouragement make it all possible.

Important Disclaimer

Mountain biking is a potentially dangerous sport in which serious injury and death can and do occur. Trails have numerous hazards, both natural and manmade, and conditions are constantly changing. Most of the routes in this book are not signed or patrolled, and this book may contain errors or omissions. It is not a substitute for proper instructions, experience and preparedness. The authors, editors, publishers and others associated with this book are not responsible for errors or omissions and do not accept liability for any loss or damage incurred from using this book. You must accept full and complete responsibility for yourself while biking in the backcountry.

Library of Congress Cataloging-in Publication Data

Bonser, Carol.
    Mountain biking the High Sierra : Lake Tahoe--south, Eldorado &
Toiyabe National Forests / by Carol Bonser & R.W. Miskimins. -- 3rd
ed.
        p.   cm.
    "Guide 3A."
    ISBN 0-938665-27-8 (paper)
    1. All terrain cycling--Tahoe, Lake, Region (Calif. and Nev.)-
-Guidebooks. 2. All terrain cycling--Sierra Nevada (Calif. and
Nev.)--Guidebooks. 3. Tahoe, Lake, Region (Calif. and Nev.)-
-Guidebooks. 4. Sierra Nevada (Calif. and Nev.)--Guidebooks.
I. Miskimins, R. W. (Ray W.) II. Title.
GV1045.5.T34B66 1993
796.6'4'0979438--dc20   93-44561
                                                                    CIP

Foreword to the First Edition

Sierra Nevada...simply to say the words conjures up adventure. Poets, mystics, thrill seekers, wanderers, and other "not quite normal" people seem to be drawn to these mountains. Today's fat tire cyclists have a lot of predecessors in these hills, and although the mode of transportation may be different, the motivation of most is the same, namely to get away from the place you are to *Someplace Else.*

The fantastic thing about this area is the variety of *Someplace Elses.* In the space of twenty air miles you can go from scrub to high alpine boulder fields, and along the way experience dense forests, alpine meadows, and glacier-carved lakes. This variety of terrain has its advantages beyond the aesthetic. The simple fact is that for most of the year *today* is a good day for a ride somewhere in this area. Cool and windy? Ride low on the south slopes. Too hot? Go high. Too muddy? It may be frozen on the north side of the mountain. Single-track? It's there all right, but some of the best rides are in places where you would least expect them. Like an old wagon road first carved into the mountains by the emigrants of 1849, only a stone's throw from Pollock Pines.

The sheer quantity of riding can overwhelm first time visitors. There is no *other side* to come out of most of the time.This book is only an introduction, and believe me, there is plenty out there for you to find on your own.

Gordon Bonser
Pollock Pines, California
October 1988

Publisher's Foreword to the Third Edition

Many changes have occurred in the Lake Tahoe region since Carol Bonser wrote this best-seller over five years ago, a fairly long time in the short history of mountain biking. Since then there have been new dirt roads built, a major forest fire, and bridges destroyed. Some trails have been closed to bikes, but others have been opened or reopened thanks to the hard work of a number of dedicated cyclists.

This all-new third edition is designed to keep you up-to-date as well as introduce you to the best of the dirt roads and trails of the Eldorado, Toiyabe and Tahoe National Forests. This edition has an additional 32 pages with new and updated routes, new computer-generated maps, and appendices covering mountain biking techniques and bike maintenance.

We are particularly glad to have Ray Miskimins, author and owner of a bicycle shop in Reno, join with Carol Bonser in updating the information on some of the finest mountain biking routes in the nation. We hope their spirit for exploration and adventure will serve you well in finding your *Someplace Else.*

Don and Réanne Douglass
Bishop, California
March 1994

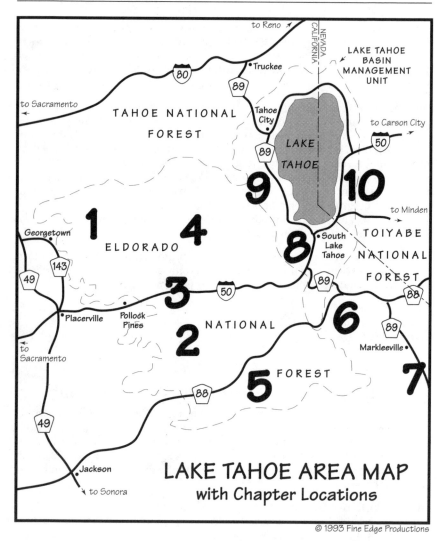

LAKE TAHOE AREA MAP
with Chapter Locations

© 1993 Fine Edge Productions

Credits

Photographs by Bette E. Miskimins, R. W. Miskimins and Carol Bonser
Book design, layout, and computer-generated maps by Sue Irwin
Original maps by Carol Bonser and R. W. Miskimins
Cover art by Bill Kelsey
Edited by Réanne Douglass

TABLE OF CONTENTS

Introduction

From the foothills on the western slope of the Sierra Nevada, eastward to the high country of the Lake Tahoe Basin, and southeast to the Toiyabe Forest along the Nevada border, the areas described in this guidebook provide some of the most extensive, varied and beautiful mountain bike riding in the country. Located just four hours east of the San Francisco Bay Area and two hours east of Sacramento, you can find rides for every season of the year and for every level of ability and interest.

Following the chapters in this book from west to east you can begin your rides in the foothills of the Sierra in late autumn and winter on dirt logging roads that wind through oak and pine forests. As spring and summer temperatures rise, you can work your way eastward to the higher elevations, riding on jeep roads and trails that take you to the very edge of four Wilderness Areas— Granite Chief, Desolation Valley, Mokelumne and the Carson Iceberg (mountain biking is illegal within the wilderness areas). In June, July and August, you can still enjoy fields of flowers that you saw at lower elevations in April and May and find relief from lowland temperatures.

If you choose the right time to visit, the foothills will be full of pink dogwoods or brilliant yellow big-leaf maples. In autumn, aspen in the high country and eastern slopes of Hope Valley and Markleeville range from shades of yellow to gold and bright orange. And since this area has usually received its first rain storm, dust is at a minimum, and riding is fantastic. For a special fall treat, try some of the rides on Monitor Pass in Chapter 7—an area famous for its small creek canyons filled with aspen.

The rides in the special chapters on the South Lake Tahoe Recreation Area offer you a chance to see just how big and beautiful the lake really is. Over the past decade, the Lake Tahoe area has become one of the most popular locations for mountain biking in the entire western United States.

This is a huge geographical area to try to cover in just one guidebook, but our intent is to give you enough background information and rides to stimulate your interest. Guide 3A covers all of Eldorado National Forest, the Lake Tahoe Basin Management Unit (within Tahoe National Forest) and parts of Toiyabe National Forest. For those interested in the Tahoe and Toiyabe National Forests see *Guide 3B, Lake Tahoe—North*.

The best part of mountain biking is the exploration and discovery of something new—a spring meadow full of flowers; a hidden stretch of single-track; a slope of golden aspen in the fall; a small creek leading down a deep ravine. These are only a few of the surprises awaiting you as you ride through these areas on your own, using this book as your guide. Enjoy your riding, and let this be just a beginning for your exploration!

Rest stop at the beach, Lake Tahoe

Special Considerations

Guide 3A covers the Eldorado National Forest, parts of the Toiyabe National Forest and the southern portion of the Lake Tahoe Basin Management Unit. The National Forest Lands within this area start in the foothills at 3,000 feet, rising to nearly 10,000 in the mountains with wide ranges in climate and weather conditions.

1. **Courtesy.** Know and follow the IMBA Rules of the Trail printed in Appendix A. Extend courtesy to all other trail users and follow the golden rule. The trails and roads in these areas are used by fishermen, hunters, horseback riders, loggers and hikers, who all feel proprietary about the use of the trails. Remember that mountain bikes are the newcomers.

2. **Preparations.** Plan your trip carefully by using a check list. Know your abilities and your equipment. Prepare to be self-sufficient at all times. Regular maintenance and a pre-ride checkup for your bike can save a lot of grief if you break down 10 or 15 miles from civilization (see Appendix B). For a discussion of recommended tools to carry, see #9 in this section and Appendix D.

3. **Mountain Conditions.** Know how to deal with dehydration, hypothermia, altitude sickness, sunburn or heatstroke. Be sensitive at all times to the natural environment—the land can be frightening and unforgiving. If you break down, it may take you much longer to walk out than it took you to ride in! Check mountaineering books and the Red Cross or Sierra Club for detailed survival information. Be particularly prepared for the following:
• *Sun:* Many of the high country rides travel over granite rocks which, in terms of reflected light, can be compared to riding across a snowfield. Protect your skin against the sun's harmful rays. Use sunscreen with a high sun protection factor ("spf"). Don't forget your eyes! Wear sunglasses with 100 UV protection. If you don't like to ride with tinted lenses, you can now buy clear lenses with 100 UV protection. Avoid lenses made of glass.
• *Low Humidity:* Start each trip with a minimum of two full quart water bottles or more. *Gallons* of water may not be sufficient for really hot weather. Force yourself to drink, whether or not you feel thirsty. Untreated drinking water may cause Giardiasis or other diseases, so carry plenty of water from a known source, or treat it.
• *Variations in Temperature and Weather Conditions:* Never travel to the high country without being prepared for afternoon thundershowers. It is not uncommon to get a brief hailstorm in mid-summer! Carry extra clothing— a windbreaker, gloves, etc.—and use the multi-layer system so you can adjust according to conditions. Keep an eye on changing cloud and wind conditions. Wind, as well as other changes in weather, can deplete your energy.

4. **Horses and Pack Animals.** Many of the trails described in this guide are used by recreational horse riders. Some horses are spooked easily, so make

them aware of your presence well in advance of the encounter. If you come upon horses moving toward you, yield the right-of-way, even when it seems inconvenient. Carry your bike to the downhill side and stand quietly, well off the trail in a spot where the animals can see you clearly. A startled horse can cause serious injuries both to an inexperienced rider and to itself. If you come upon horses moving ahead of you in the same direction, stop well behind them. Do not attempt to pass until you have alerted the riders and asked for permission. Then, pass as quietly as you can on the downhill side of the trail. It is *your* responsibility to ensure that such encounters are safe for everyone!

5. Respect the Environment. Minimize your impact on the natural environment. *Remember, mountain bikes are not allowed in designated Wilderness Areas, on the Pacific Crest Trail and in certain other restricted areas.* Ask, when in doubt. You are a visitor. Leave plants and animals alone, historic and cultural sites untouched. Stay on established roads and trails, and do not enter private property. Follow posted instructions and use good common sense. *Note:* If you plan to camp within a National Forest you need a Campfire Permit to have a fire or to use a stove outside of a campground. For information on permits, regulations and seasonal fire closures, contact the Eldorado National Forest Service at (916) 644-6048. To report fires call (702) 883-5995—a 24-hour Inter-Agency Dispatch Center.

6. Control and Safety. Keep your bike in control at all times. Guard against excessive speed. Avoid overheated rims and brakes on long or steep downhill rides. Lower your center of gravity by lowering your seat on downhills. Lower your tire pressure on rough or sandy stretches. (See Appendix C for a description of basic mountain biking skills.) Avoid the opening weekend of hunting season (ask local sporting goods stores which areas are open to hunting). Don't ride by yourself in remote areas. Carry first aid supplies and bike tools for emergencies.

Most crashes don't cause serious injury, but they can and do. Stay under control and slow for the unexpected. Wear protective gear—helmet, leather gloves, over-the-ankle boots, long pants, or tights—to protect yourself. Most serious cycling injuries are to the head. Give up your body to road rash if you choose, but protect your head with a fully approved (Snell and ANSI) helmet!

7. First Aid and Safety. Always carry a first-aid kit—several companies market kits specifically designed for cyclists. If you have allergies be sure to bring your medicine, whether it's for pollen or bee stings. Remember that sluggish or cramping muscles and fatigue indicate dehydration and/or the need for calories. Carry plenty of water and high-energy snack foods such as granola bars, dried fruits and nuts to maintain strength and warmth; add clothing layers as the temperature drops or the wind increases. Also be aware of the following:
• *Black bears* may be out and about. Food seems to cause the most problems,

so a clean camp is advised.
• *Rattlesnakes* can be startling and are dangerous at close range, but they are usually noisy when alarmed and retreat readily. Snakes are most often seen in the lower elevations, close to a water source, hidden in the rocks. Most snake bites are reported in April, May and early June when the snakes lie in the sun trying to warm up. Later on in the summer, they will be hiding in the shade, and you probably won't see them.
• *Mosquitoes and deerflies* are more of an annoyance than a true health hazard. If the mosquitoes like you, carry insect repellent when riding, especially during the months of May through July.
• *Poison oak* is usually found in this area at 4,000 feet and below. The plant—sometimes a bush and other times vine-like—is recognized by its oak-like leaves in groups of three along the stems. It has an oil that causes rashes with blistering one to five days after contact. Avoid direct contact with any part of the plant, contact with an animal that has brushed against it, contact with clothing or gloves that have touched it, or inhalation of smoke from a burning plant. Wash immediately to prevent or lessen the rash. For more severe cases see your doctor.

8. **Maps & Navigation.** Everyone who enjoys exploring by mountain bike should know how to read a map and use a compass. The maps in this book are designed to be used with National Forest Maps and U.S. Geological Survey Maps (USGS topo maps). A legal description (location) is given for the starting point of each area—for example, T9N R14E, section 10 is the location of the Capp's Crossing Campground, a good place to camp and ride. Maps are made up of grids. Across the top and bottom of the Eldorado National Forest Map are the numbers R10E to R19E, for Range 10 East to Range 19 East. Vertically on the left and right are T7N to T15N, for Township 7 North to Township 15 North. Using the legal description for Capp's Crossing, find where T9N and R14E cross, forming a large square made up of smaller squares, called sections. Each section is numbered from 1-36. You should now have no problem locating Capp's Crossing within section 10.

Warning: Not all roads on the USFS maps are on the guidebook maps, and not all roads found on the maps in this guidebook are on the USFS maps!

The handiest maps to use while riding are the USGS topo maps, 7.5 minute series. They maps are more recent than the 15 minute series and tend to show many of the newer roads. Everything you learned about the legal descriptions is the same for the topo maps, the squares are just larger. Each section of the maps represents one square mile.

Another hint: Have you ever noticed trees in the forest that have yellow tags nailed onto their trunk? If you haven't, keep your eyes open from now on. These tags are called K-Tags. On each K-Tag is one complete Township with 36 sections. On the top or bottom of the tag will be the Township and Range numbers. Then there should be one nail hole in a section square indicating the section you're in. Look on your map and you can quickly find out where you are!

It's easy to get lost. Before you leave on a trip, tell someone where you are going, with whom you are riding, when you expect to return, and what to do in case you don't return on time. Ask them to call the El Dorado County Sheriff if you are more than six hours overdue, giving full details about your vehicle and your trip plans. While you're en route, keep track of your position on your trip map(s). Record the time you arrive at a known place on the map. Be sure to look back frequently in the direction from which you came, in case you need to retrace your path. Don't be afraid to turn back when conditions change, or when the going is rougher than you expected.

In case of emergency, call the El Dorado County Central Dispatch (916) 622-1112, or 911 in El Dorado County or Alpine County.

9. **Trailside Bike Repair.** Minimum equipment: pump, spare tube, patches, 2 tubes of patch glue, 6" adjustable wrench, Allen wrenches, chain tool and a spoke wrench (see Appendix D). Tools may be shared with others in your group. Correct inflation, wide tires, and avoiding rocks will prevent most flats. Grease, oil, and proper maintenance prevent almost all mechanical failures.

1 GEORGETOWN AREA / RUBICON RIVER CANYON

Bald Mountain Orientation Loop;
Bald Mountain Short Loop;
Ellicott's Crossing/Hunter's Trail; Camp Seven Loop

The Drive: Take U.S. 50 east to Placerville, turn left (north) on Highway 49. About one mile later, turn right on Highway 193 (follow signs to Georgetown). This highway drops down into the American River Canyon and crosses the river at Chili Bar. This is the put-in point for rafts and kayaks rafting the upper section of the South Fork of the American River. Continue on Highway 193 up out of the canyon to Georgetown. (From Interstate 80, go east to Auburn, south on Highway 49, to Pilot Hill, then east on Highway 193 to Georgetown.)

Turn right (northeast) onto Main Street in Georgetown. If you need supplies, groceries, gas, etc., stop here. This is the last major town before you enter the National Forest. A word of caution regarding driving through Georgetown—it is legal to park in the center divider of Main Street in both directions. At times it seems that cars are coming at you from all directions! Continue on Main Street, which becomes Wentworth Springs Road, as soon as you leave town. About 3 miles out of town on your right is the U.S Forest Service Georgetown Ranger Station. If you don't have a map, stop here to pick up a USFS Road Map. (Also available is an excellent packet called "Hiking Trails of the Georgetown Area, Eldorado National Forest.")

ROCK CREEK RECREATIONAL AREA   *Map 1*

3.2 miles farther (6.2 miles from Georgetown), turn right on Balderston Road, then veer left onto Mace Mill Road, follow the signs and either ride or drive out to OHV staging area. This area is part of a 22,000 acre Recreational Trails Area for Off-Highway Vehicles that has been developed by the Forest Service with State OHV funding money. A controversy has sprung up between motorcycle clubs, horseback riders and environmental groups, with mountain bikers caught in the middle of it all. Right now, funding for further work on the project has stopped, with everything on hold until the controversy is resolved. The area is open, but no further development is taking place.

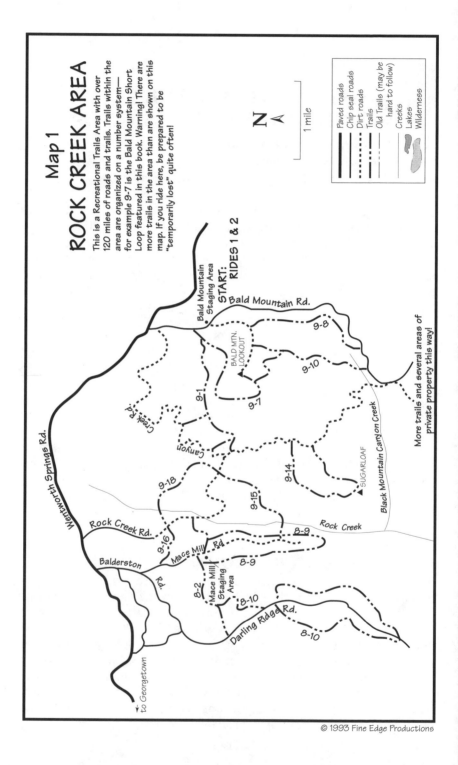

Map 1
ROCK CREEK AREA

This is a Recreational Trails Area with over 120 miles of roads and trails. Trails within the area are organized on a number system—for example 9-7 is the Bald Mountain Short Loop featured in this book. Warning! There are more trails in the area than are shown on this map. If you ride here, be prepared to be "temporarily lost" quite often!

N

1 mile

| Paved roads |
| Chip seal roads |
| Dirt roads |
| Trails |
| Old Trails (may be hard to follow) |
| Creeks |
| Lakes |
| Wilderness |

Bald Mountain Staging Area

START:
RIDES 1 & 2

Bald Mountain Rd.

BALD MTN. LOOKOUT

9-8

9-10

9-1

9-7

Canyon Creek Rd.

SUGARLOAF

Black Mountain Canyon Creek

More trails and several areas of private property this way!

9-18

9-14

9-15

Rock Creek Rd.

9-16

Mace Mill Rd.

8-9

Rock Creek

Balderston

8-9

8-2

Mace Mill Staging Area

8-10

Darling Ridge Rd.

8-10

Rd.

Wentworth Springs Rd.

to Georgetown

You can ride your mountain bike here on 85 miles of trails and 35 miles of dirt road. Stop at the Georgetown Ranger Station for an excellent map of the Rock Creek OHV area. The Mace Mill staging area is at 3,200' and below, which means it is a great spot for winter training rides. It is usually rideable, except during or immediately following a storm (this area gets 50 to 60 inches of rain per year!). This is a great spot for the novice or expert riders to work on bike handling skills. Trails vary from straightforward single-track, to difficult trials sections. You may want to stop and practice some sections again to build up your skills.

After 9.8 miles (3.6 miles past Mace Mill Road) on Wentworth Springs Road, turn right at the sign *Bald Mountain Lookout 2 miles; Rock Creek Road 5 miles; Five Corners 5 miles* and drive out 1/2 mile to the Bald Mountain staging area. This is another part of the Rock Creek Recreational Area, with trails everywhere. If you have more than one day to ride, try the Loop Ride first, to orient yourself. Many of the trails end or cross this loop, so if you do this ride first, you'll know how to get back to your car without pushing up a trail.

Ride 1   Bald Mountain Orientation Loop

Topo Map: 7.5 min. Georgetown & Tunnel Hill; 15 min. Georgetown & Saddle Mountain. Start: T12N, R11E, section 1.
Total Mileage: 13.5 miles.
Water: Available only down in the creek drainages. If you stay up on the ridges carry all that you think you will need.
Level of Difficulty: This is an easy ride, half on a paved road, and the rest on dirt.
Elevation: 3,200'–4,400'.
Seasons: Year-round, except after a heavy rain or occasional low elevation snow. It can be very hot in the summer.
Camping: The closest Forest Service Campground is located 6 miles east on Wentworth Springs Road at Stumpy Meadows Lake.

The Ride: From the staging area, ride back to the paved road and turn right at the sign that says *Rock Creek Road 5 miles.* The entire first 5 miles is on a paved road that winds in and out of the canyons, goes around the ridge, then downhill to an intersection. Turn right, the road straight ahead is Ballarat Trail, marked as a jeep trail. Several longer loops can be ridden from here. Continue on the main road, paying attention to the trail crossing signs, as these are the OHV trails coming down from Bald Mountain Lookout and the ridge where you parked your car. 3 miles: Turn right at the sign that says *Quintette 5 miles.* Some spots of this trail pass through Southern Pacific private land. *Stay on the road!* After 3 miles, the road begins to deteriorate and becomes quite rutted. 0.5 later, continue right on the main road 1.5 miles, and you have reached the Wentworth Springs Road. Turn right and follow the signs back to Bald Mountain Staging Area, where you parked your car.

Ride 2   Bald Mountain Short Loop

Mileage: 5 miles
Level of Difficulty: Easy ride, except for the one rocky downhill, but that section is so short, you can walk it if you choose. Note: The Bald Mountain Area is covered with trails for all ability levels.

The Ride: From the staging area, ride out the road, or the trail that parallels the road to Bald Mountain Lookout. 1.0 mile, turn right at the sign that says *Bald Mt. 1/2 mile.* Or, for a gonzo downhill—experts only!—go straight ahead for 1+ mile onto a loosely rocked and rutted trail This ties in with Loop Ride 1, at the 4 mile mark. 0.5 miles later, at the tower, walk around and orient yourself with your map. Ride over to the radio tower and look for a trail that goes along the fence line (on the left side). Go down this trail and to the right. Ride out the ridge to the first trail that doubles back to the left. This trail goes back under the lookout tower, then dives off for a fast, rough downhill section. Don't panic! It's less than a half mile long! At the four way intersection, the left trail goes a ways out on the contour, then dives off. The trail straight ahead dives off quickly for more downhill and eventually ties in with Loop Ride 1. Go right to complete the short loop. The next 2 miles is on an old railroad grade, fun and easy trail riding. 2.0 miles, and the end of the trail. Turn right at the paved road. Up ahead is Bald Mountain Staging Area and your car.

One last comment about riding this area—although the lower sections of the Mace Mill Road rides could be considered almost year round rides, the farther you go out Wentworth Springs Road, the higher the elevation. This road is not plowed in the winter and opens in the spring, after the snow melts.

RUBICON RIVER CANYON   *Map 2*
Ellicott's Crossing/Hunter's Trail

The Rubicon River canyon is spectacular, with sections of steep granite gorge and beautiful deep pools. If you enjoy fishing and swimming plan extra time to hike down to the river.
Nearest Services: 28 miles back to Georgetown for groceries, gas etc. A

small store is also located 6 miles away at Uncle Tom's Cabin. *Campgrounds:* Forest Service Campground at Stumpy Meadows, 10 miles back toward Georgetown. Dispersed camping is allowed along the river, with a campfire permit. Be extremely careful with fire here, as it can be very hot and the tinder dry by early June! Be sure to stop at the Ranger Station to check on current fire restrictions.

The Drive: From Georgetown, go east on Wentworth Springs Road 23 miles to the intersection of Uncle Tom's Cabin Road. Go left toward Hell Hole. The road drops quickly into the Rubicon River Canyon. Go 5 miles to the bottom, to a giant bridge. This is Ellicott's Crossing. The ride starts on the far side of the bridge. Parking is available where you first reach the bridge on the left or right side. Park here if you have a new car, one with low clearance or one that doesn't go up or down steep, rocky hills. There are campsites available by the Rubicon River, down the rough road. Go across the bridge and take the first road on the right that takes you down to the river. 0.2 miles down, look left and you can see a sign marked *Rubicon Trail, Hale's Crossing 4 miles; Hell Hole Reservoir 10 miles.* (Rubicon Trail is called Hunter's Trail on USGS topo maps and in "Hiking Trails of the Georgetown Area.") Note: At the time of this writing, Hunter's Trail is temporarily closed (to study "unsurveyed archaeological sites"). Call the U.S Forest Service Georgetown Ranger Station (916-333-4312) to determine current status.

USGS Topos: 7.5 min. Robb's Peak, Bunker Hill; 15 min. Robb's Peak; Granite Chief. Start: T13N, R13E, section 23
Water: The trail follows the Rubicon River all the way, so water is not a problem, as long as you have a filter to purify your supply.
Level of Difficulty: Advanced and expert riders. Do not ride this trail if you have never done any mountain bike trail riding—it is for advanced and expert riders! The trail is narrow and the river canyon drops off steeply in many places. Everyone will walk their bike in spots on the way up the canyon and even on the way out. If you do this ride, tell someone where you are going and when you plan to return. If someone gets hurt, it is up to the rest of your riding group to get help.
Elevation: The start at Ellicott's Crossing 3,300'; Parsley Bar—upper end 4,200'. (If you ride the trail past Parsley Bar to Hell Hole, you climb to 5,200' or 5,600', depending on which trail you choose.)
Seasons: Best in April and May, whenever the road opens, or after the first rain in the fall. It is rideable all summer long, but the canyon can be extremely hot!

The Ride: The route is simple to follow. Go out the Rubicon Trail mentioned earlier in *The Drive* section. The first mile is the toughest. You wind in and out of creek canyons and be off your bike, pushing up some

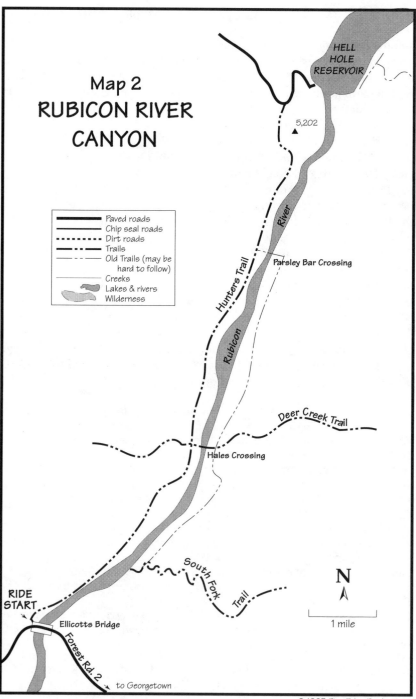

Map 2
RUBICON RIVER
CANYON

HELL HOLE RESERVOIR

5,202

River

Parsley Bar Crossing

Hunters Trail

Rubicon

Deer Creek Trail

Hales Crossing

South Fork Trail

N

1 mile

RIDE START

Ellicotts Bridge

Forest Rd. 2

to Georgetown

Paved roads
Chip seal roads
Dirt roads
Trails
Old Trails (may be hard to follow)
Creeks
Lakes & rivers
Wilderness

short steep sections. At 0.3 mile a trail comes in from above, go straight. At 1.2 miles a trail comes in from above. Sign: *Grey Trail; Nevada Point Road 3 miles.* Nevada Point Road at the end of Grey Trail is at 5,300'. This means a climb of over 2,000' to get out of this canyon! A trail to try *down*, not up! At 2.3 miles, you come to an old cabin site, and 0.2 mile farther you arrive at Hale's Crossing, signed: *Hale's Crossing and Rim Road.* If you look on the back of the tree behind the sign, you can see an old Forest Service sign: *Grizzly Ranch, 8 miles [right]; Jerry's Pool, 5 miles [right].* Jerry's Pool is a small lake. Though there is very little use in this area now, the old trail signs along this canyon show this was once a major trail for the gold miners who worked along the Rubicon River. Walk down to the river and you should be able to see where the early settlers used to cross.

After you've done your exploring, continue on 1.5 miles, and you will find more old trail signs. *Big Meadows 5 miles [right]; Hell Hole 6 1/2 miles [right]; Hales Camp Trail, and Hales Camp 2 miles.* After about 1/2 mile, the trail falls apart—it is rocky, washed out and, naturally, it just happens to be out in full sun. You will begin to question riding any farther, but there is good riding ahead. And yes, it is worth pushing on! Pay attention to the trail, you can often ride down the rough stuff you had to push up. 1.5 miles past the rough section, you will see a "K tag" (yellow tag on sign post) that says you are in T14N R14E, at the corner of section 20, 21 / 29,28. This means you are at the upper end of Parsley Bar. You have travelled 7 1/2 miles so far. Parsley Bar is located to your right, along the river. Ride and walk out to see where the river has deposited an amazing

Rubicon River Canyon

pile of rocks of all sizes, from sand to very large boulders! From Parsley Bar, the trail goes up the drainage and climbs to over 5,000' up to Hell Hole Reservoir, in about 2 miles (climbing 1,000' from where you are now). The coming down is fun, but going up is work.

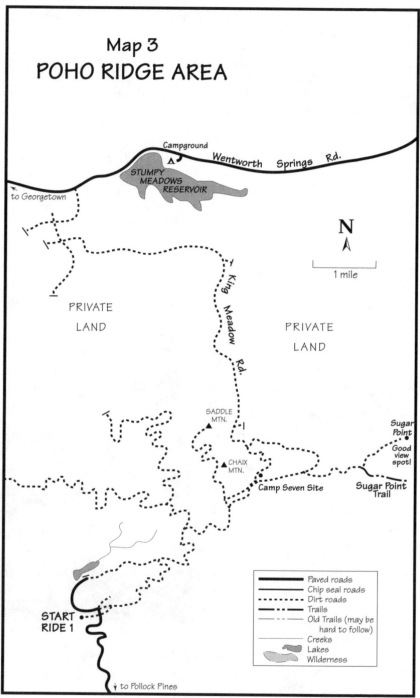

Map 3
POHO RIDGE AREA

Campground

Wentworth Springs Rd.

STUMPY MEADOWS RESERVOIR

to Georgetown

N

1 mile

King Meadow Rd.

PRIVATE LAND

PRIVATE LAND

SADDLE MTN.

CHAIX MTN.

Sugar Point

Good view spot!

Camp Seven Site

Sugar Point Trail

START RIDE 1

to Pollock Pines

	Paved roads
	Chip seal roads
	Dirt roads
	Trails
	Old Trails (may be hard to follow)
	Creeks
	Lakes
	Wilderness

© 1993 Fine Edge Productions

After a rest and a swim, follow the trail back to Ellicott's Crossing. Going in the downstream direction, you will understand why mountain bikers like this trail. So much of what you had to walk, you can now ride. In this direction, you may not walk at all. Total miles: 15.5. A good, deep swimming hole is located just downstream from the bridge.

There is a maze of trails in this river canyon for you to explore. The most rideable in both directions is the Hunter's Trail (described above). South Fork, Deer Creek and Parsley Bar are all accessed from the Ice House Road, off Highway 50. Be sure to check the topos so you know the elevation drop before you head down these trails.

POHO RIDGE *Map 3*

Poho Ridge is a southern portion of the area known as the Georgetown Divide. While other parts of El Dorado County were filling up with mining communities, the Divide was being settled by those in the timber industry. During the early 1900s the Divide was covered with railroad lines running between the logging camps and the main sawmill located at Pino Grande. Many of the logging camps (named by numbers, Camp 7, Camp 9, etc.) were accessible only by railroad.

In the 1940s, the switch began from railroads to roads and logging trucks. Many of the roads in use today follow the old railroad lines which makes for some great mountain bike rides. Part of the fun of this area is in the exploration of the old railroad grades. They are everywhere! Many of them are in rideable condition, while others are overgrown and covered with downed timber. Much of the riding on Poho Ridge is on south-facing slopes, which means a long riding season. Some of the rides stay on the sunny side and could be considered year-round rides, except, of course, during and immediately following heavy rain storms or low elevation snow storms. The best riding seasons are March through May, and September through mid-November.

The Drive: Although considered part of the Georgetown Ranger District (and accessible by taking San Mountain Road off of Wentworth Road), the easiest route to this Forest Service land is from Pollock Pines. Take U.S. 50 east of Pollock Pines. Take the Sly Park off-ramp, turn left under the freeway. At the stop sign, turn left again (west) on Pony Express Trail. Just past the mini-storage units, turn right on Forebay Road. Stay on this road, past the reservoir, along the ridge, then down to the bottom of the river canyon. Cross the south fork of the American River and drive to the top of the ridge. Park in the big flat area at the top. This drive is 13.5 miles from U.S. 50.

Topo maps: 7.5 min. Pollock Pines & Devil Peak; 15 min. Saddle Mountain. All rides begin at the top of the ridge T11N, R12E, section 15.

Water: Carry plenty! Although there are several small creeks, it is not wise to count on them as a water supply; many will be dry by the end of June.

Nearest Services: Take everything you will need with you, even though you are only 13.5 miles away from town; this is another part of the forest that is seldom used. The nearest *anything* is back at Pollock Pines.

Camp Seven Loop

Mileage: 18.5 miles.
Elevation: 3,300'–4,680'.
Level of Difficulty: For intermediate or better riders—it is a medium length ride with a good amount of climbing in the first 5.4 miles to Camp Seven. Once you reach the 4,500' level at Camp Seven, the loop ride is on railroad grade, with gradual gains and loss of elevation. All road surfaces are good, meaning fairly smooth dirt!

The Ride: Take the road that heads east along the top of Poho Ridge. Follow the sign that says *Camp Seven 9 miles* (don't believe it, it's not that far). Stay on the main road. 3.8 miles out, turn right following the sign that says *Camp Seven 2 miles* (this time you can believe the sign!). After riding up 2 miles more, you arrive at the remains of Camp Seven, the site of a busy, summer logging community during the early 1900s. Continue straight ahead through the camp following the railroad grade out the ridge. 0.6 mile, when you reach a three way intersection, go straight ahead to ride to Sugar Pine Point, go left for a shorter loop; the road to the right dead-ends.

Go straight ahead to Sugar Pine Point. (0.8 mile out on the right is a sign pointing the way to *Sugar Point Trail; 2 miles to Big Silver Creek.*) *Warning:* This trail drops straight down into the river canyon. Continue on the main road 0.7 mile farther, where the road ends at Sugar Pine Point. Ride until the road drops straight off, then walk down to the tower to see just how steep the canyon is! Jay Bird Reservoir is just below you. If you look straight out you should see Big Hill Lookout—the towers you see on the ridge in line with Pyramid Peak. This is a good lunch spot. After lunch, ride back to the three-way intersection, this time turn right.

Enjoy some more downhill. Then after 2.0 miles of a gradual climb, turn left following the sign that reads: *Camp Seven 1 mile [left]; Locked Gate [right]*. It is an easy climb to 4,680' elevation, then enjoy the downhill back to Camp Seven. Turn right at Camp Seven, then enjoy 5.4 miles of mostly downhill back to your car!

More on Poho Ridge

This area was logged during the summer of 1988. There are now several new roads to ride, as long as you don't mind riding through clear cuts. Another suggestion for rides in this area is to locate Slate Mountain and Big X Mountain on your Forest Service Map (northwest from where you parked your car). Several ride options are available in that direction. Most of the land between Poho Ridge and the Wentworth Springs Road is private and closed to public use. The only road open to the public at this time that travels to Wentworth Springs is the Sand Mountain Road. (Look for the solid double line road on your Forest Service Map.) Don't let all of this discourage you. There is plenty of land out here, and remember it is a great place to ride during the winter!

Lake Tahoe Fire Road

Map 4: PARK CREEK/PLUM CREEK AREA

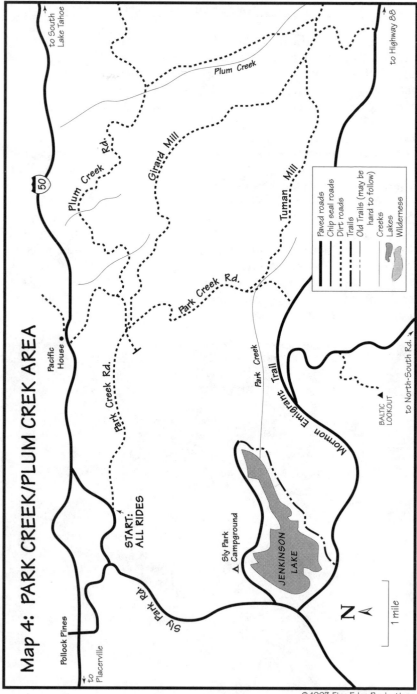

to South Lake Tahoe

Plum Creek

Plum Creek Rd.

Girard Mill

50

Tuman Mill

to Highway 88

Pacific House

Park Creek Rd.

Park Creek Rd.

Park Creek

Mormon Emigrant Trail

to North-South Rd.

BALTIC LOOKOUT

START: ALL RIDES

Pollock Pines

to Placerville

Sly Park Rd.

Sly Park Campground

JENKINSON LAKE

N

1 mile

Legend
Paved roads
Chip seal roads
Dirt roads
Trails
Old Trails (may be hard to follow)
Creeks
Lakes
Wilderness

2 POLLOCK PINES / IRON MOUNTAIN ROAD
(Mormon Emigrant Trail)

CHAPTER

Plum Creek Out and Back; Tuman Mill/Plum Creek Loop; Girard Mill Hill Climb; Snow Mill/Pebble Canyon Loop; Meiss Cabin/Baltic Ridge Loop; The Ridge Ride; Camp Creek Loop; Alder Ridge Lookout Loop; Alder/Oso Springs Loop; Alder Ridge/Ridge Ride

Three hours from the San Francisco Bay Area and one hour from Sacramento, travelling east on U.S. Highway 50, you reach the town of Pollock Pines on the edge of the Eldorado National Forest. This is the last major town with gas stations, motels and all-night grocery stores. Get your supplies before heading into the forest.

Radiating from Pollock Pines on Mormon Emigrant Trail you will find endless logging roads where you can easily design your own rides of 10 to 40 miles, all on dirt surfaces! The area along the Mormon Emigrant Trail was a major route for the early pioneers coming into California in 1848. Look for the monuments—they are made of railroad iron painted a rust color, placed along the Mormon-Carson-Emigrant Trail by Oregon Trails West, Inc. If you see one, take time to stop and read it.

Mormon Emigrant Trail is known by the locals as the Iron Mountain Road. If you use 7.5 min. topo maps, the road is called Iron Mountain Road. If you look on a 15 min. topo map, the road is called Silver Lake Road. Very few people call this Silver Lake Road anymore, but Iron Mountain Road is quite common. In this chapter we use Mormon Emigrant Trail because the newer Forest Service signs are now labeled this way. The elevation along the road ranges from 3,800' to 7,600'. High enough so that those of you from the flatlands will feel it, but not so high that you'll feel like your lungs are going to explode.

Warning: Mormon Emigrant Trail is a wonderful short cut to Highway 88 and the Carson Pass Area. This road does not get plowed in winter, but after a dry winter it is usually open by the end of May. In a year with a wet winter it can be as late as early July. When you exit Highway 50 at Sly Park, look for a sign that tells you if the road is open or closed. The area is a prime timber area for the U.S. Forest Service and private

Sierra trailhead

land owners. This not only means new roads to explore every year but also that you need to respect signs that say *Timber Falling Ahead*. Sometimes, a road may be closed for safety. At other times, it's just a matter of making sure whoever is in charge of the area sees you and tells you when it is safe to travel through.

Water is available in the numerous creeks but should be treated, boiled or filtered before you drink it. Certain rides have few or no water stops; this will be mentioned at the beginning of each ride. The riding at lower elevations—Park Creek/Plum Creek Area is usually good all year round. The exception is the 10 to 20 days a year when there is snow on the ground or immediately following a downpour.

PARK CREEK/PLUM CREEK AREA   *Map 4*

The Drive: From Placerville go east on U.S. 50 to Pollock Pines. Take the Sly Park Road offramp at the east end of town. Turn right (go south) on Sly Park Road. At 1.6 miles turn left on Park Creek Road, drive until the pavement ends (0.5 mile). There is plenty of parking available here, just be sure not to block the entrance to the Wood Lot.

Topo Maps: 7.5 min. Pollock Pines, Riverton, Camino, and Sly Park. 15 min. Saddle Mountain, Robbs Peak, Leek Springs Hill and Camino. All rides on Map 4 start: T11N, R13E, section 32.

Campgrounds: Three miles farther downhill on Sly Park Road is Sly Park Campground at Jenkinson Lake, open year-round for boating, fishing, hiking, etc. It's a great place to stay or picnic after a ride. Some of the trails in the campground are open to mountain bikes, including one along the lake shore. Ask at the gate for a map and current information on bike trails.

Nearest Services: Small store and bar located across from the entrance to the campground. Grocery stores, gas stations, motels and restaurants are located in Pollock Pines.

Ride 1 Plum Creek Out and Back

Mileage: 21 miles total.
Water: Usually available at Plum Creek until late summer. In a dry year carry all you will need. Filter or treat all the water you take from the stream.
Level of Difficulty: Easy—if an easy 21-mile-long mountain bike ride exists. This is a good ride to introduce people to mountain bike riding without burning them out. One section of the road is chip seal surface—smooth riding along the edge of the American River Canyon. To shorten the ride, drive your car 2.5 miles farther to Five Corners.
Elevation: 4200' with very little loss or gain.

The Ride: Everyone can enjoy this ride; better riders just ride faster! Ride out the dirt Park Creek Road (green signs help here) 2.5 miles to Five Corners, an intersection where five roads meet. **Warning:** Do not take the immediate right to Hazel Creek Mine—they don't appreciate visitors. The road to the right is the continuation of Park Creek Road. The road straight ahead is Girard Mill Road. (Look for the Oregon Trails West marker to read about the pioneers of 1848!) The road to the left is Plum Creek Road, go left!

Stay on the main road all the way, always straight ahead at basically the same elevation. Roads to the right are usually steep and they dead-end quickly. Roads to the left (downhill) end at the PG&E ditch or Highway 50. **Warning:** The PG&E ditch may look like an inviting place to get wet. Stay out of the ditch! The water is much deeper and the current a lot stronger than it looks. 2.3 miles: Continue straight ahead, road to the left goes to Pacific House (Highway 50). 1.2 miles: You cross Ogilby Creek, and many first timers turn around here. Total miles: 6 one way, 12 round trip. Climb to the top of the ridge, then it is basically all downhill to Plum Creek. You have now travelled 10 miles. A nice picnic spot is located across Plum Creek. Park by the big log, and walk to your left towards the stream.

The road straight ahead used to be a steep, rough, rocky route known as the Highway to Heaven. Today it is paved, provides a fast route to the top, and leads to several dirt roads for mountain bikes to explore. The road to the right is the continuation of Plum Creek Road. We call it the Upper Plum Creek Road and include it in Ride 2, Tuman Mill/Plum Creek Loop. To complete this out-and-back ride, follow your tracks to return to the car.

Ride 2   Tuman Mill/Plum Creek Loop

Mileage: 23 miles from the end of the pavement on Park Creek Road.
Level of Difficulty: Intermediate to advanced climbing, with a challenging, rutted downhill (1,000' drop in 2 miles).
Elevation: 4,200'–5,200'.

The Ride: Ride out Park Creek Road to Five Corners 2.5 miles, turn right continuing on Park Creek Road. At the top of the hill 1.4 miles later, continue on the main road. After another 1.4 miles, turn left on Tuman Mill Road. (If you miss this turn you will cross Park Creek and start to climb to Mormon Emigrant Trail, a large paved road.) 0.3 mile: Two spur roads enter from the left, continue straight ahead past a church camp on the right. 2.7 miles: Two spurs enter from the left; continue straight ahead on the main road that makes a sharp right turn, then goes left around the ridge. 0.6 mile: Take the left that continues the gradual, but steady up. 1.5 miles: Look to the left for the Oregon Trails West marker located at the intersection of Girard Mill Road. (You can go left down Girard Mill for another fun downhill run—7 miles back to Five Corners.)

To do this loop, continue straight ahead past one more spur to the left. 0.2 mile: Turn left and continue climbing. 0.5 mile: You are at the top. Go downhill, past a creek and through a large opening. 1.2 miles: Go left downhill. (If you miss this turn, you climb the ridge and end up on Mormon Emigrant Trail). This next 1.5 miles is a steep downhill, with waterbars and usually deep ruts. Take it easy and enjoy the ride down to "Bear Track Bridge" which crosses Plum Creek. No riders have reported seeing bears in this area, but several have reported footprints near or on the log bridge. 2.5 miles: Cross Plum Creek, a nice spot for a rest.

The ride from here on is a gentle gradual climb, then the road basically follows the 4,200' elevation all the way back to Five Corners. Follow the signs that tell you that you are on Plum Creek Road heading towards Park Creek Road. 8 miles: At Five Corners continue straight ahead on Park Creek Road and ride the last 2.5 miles back to the car.

Ride 3   Girard Mill Hill Climb

Mileage: 19 miles from end of pavement in Park Creek Road.
Water: None. Carry adequate supplies.
Elevation: 4,190'–5,040'.
Level of Difficulty: Intermediate Hill Climb. Good training and endurance ride.

The Ride: Ride out the dirt road (Park Creek Road) 2.5 miles to Five Corners. Look in front of you for the Oregon Trails West marker (rust colored railroad iron) that says:

> *Hazel Creek*
> *Mormon – Carson – Emigrant Trail 1848.*
> *Emigrants left their wagons on the trail here and drove stock down Hazel Creek to recuit on water and grass at Sly Park.*

Sly Park is now a reservoir; back in 1848 it was a huge meadow and settlement. You will be riding on an old wagon road up the ridge to the next historical marker at "Zumwalts." Once on Girard Mill Road the road immediately forks. Go left on the volcanic-cobbled road. Conserve your energy and continue pumping. It's never that technical; it just keeps going up! You know the hill climb is over when you reach the other historical marker "Zumwalts":

> *Zumwalts*
> *Mormon-Carson Emigrant Trail 1848*
> *Original 1848 Mormon road passes through this depression in Iron Mountain Ridge.*

Your options from here: Turn left and follow the Plum Creek loop directions. Turn right down Tuman Mill Road to Park Creek. Or, the usual route is to go back down Girard Mill. Most people feel they deserve to have some fun after the climb.

Snow Mill/Pebble Canyon Loop   *Map 5*

Topo Maps: 7.5 min. Stump Springs. Start: T10N, R13E, section 13.
Mileage: 18 miles.
Water: Available at half way point at Camp Creek. Filter or treat all water.
Elevation: 4,500–5,100'.
Level of Difficulty: Easy to intermediate—we've had several 8-year-olds complete this ride feeling like they've accomplished a lot!
Campgrounds: Camping is available year-round at Sly Park 4 miles west on Mormon Emigrant; summer camping at Capps Crossing USFS Campground. (East on Mormon Emigrant Road 6 miles, turn right on North-South Road 6 miles to campground).
Nearest Services: 10 miles back to U.S. 50 and Pollock Pines.

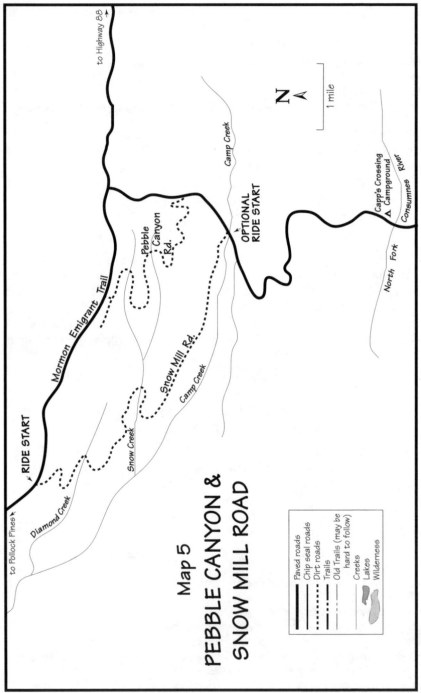

Map 5
PEBBLE CANYON &
SNOW MILL ROAD

N

1 mile

to Highway 88

to Pollock Pines

RIDE START

Mormon Emigrant Trail

Diamond Creek

Snow Creek

Snow Mill Rd.

Pebble Canyon Rd.

Camp Creek

Camp Creek

OPTIONAL RIDE START

Capp's Crossing
Campground

North Fork

Consumnes River

Paved roads
Chip seal roads
Dirt roads
Trails
Old Trails (may be hard to follow)
Creeks
Lakes
Wilderness

© 1993 Fine Edge Productions

The Drive: U.S. 50 east to Pollock Pines. Take Sly Park Road south (turn right) 4.5 miles. Turn left on Mormon Emigrant Trail. Drive 5.8 miles to Snow Mill Road and park near the green steel gate.

The Ride: Go up Mormon Emigrant Trail 3 miles to Pebble Canyon Road. Turn right on Pebble Canyon. You are faced with an immediate fork— take the immediate left. Stay on the main road for 5 miles. Turn right on paved North-South Road. Continue 1 mile to the bridge at Camp Creek. Good rest spot to swim or get water. *Remember to filter or treat all water.* Turn right (west) on the dirt road that takes off just before you cross the bridge. This is Snow Mill Road. After a short, steep rocky section the riding becomes easy again, winding in and out of the canyons. Watch out for gravelly downhill sections. Remind beginners to go easy on the front brake! Stay on the main road and you'll be back to your car 9 miles later.

CAPPS CROSSING AREA   *Map 6*

Rides 1 and 2, described in this section, are just a sample of what is available from Capps Crossing Campground—a great mountain bike campground. There is a maze of roads in all directions that still need to be explored!

The Drive: Take U.S. 50 east from Placerville to Pollock Pines. Take Sly Park Road south (turn right) 4.5 miles. Turn left on Mormon Emigrant Trail. Drive 10.8 miles to North-South Road and turn right (south). Continue 6 miles to Capps Crossing Campground. If you are planning on camping, pull into the campground and pick out a campsite. Otherwise, continue on the North-South Road across the bridge where parking is available along the side of the road.

Ride 1   Meiss Cabin/Baltic Ridge Loop

Topo Maps: 7.5 min. Stump Springs; Leek Springs Hill. 15 min. Leek Springs Hill; Silver Creek. Start: T9N, R14E, section 10.
Mileage: 18.5 miles.
Water: Capps Crossing Campground.
Level of Difficulty: Intermediate. 9 miles and 1,420' of steady climbing gain but it's all paved so it's not technical. Then it's 9 miles of downhill on an old jeep road with lots of obstacles to negotiate.
Elevation: Beginning Capps Crossing 5,180'; high point 6,600'.
Nearest Services: 22 miles back at Pollock Pines.
Seasons: May through October.

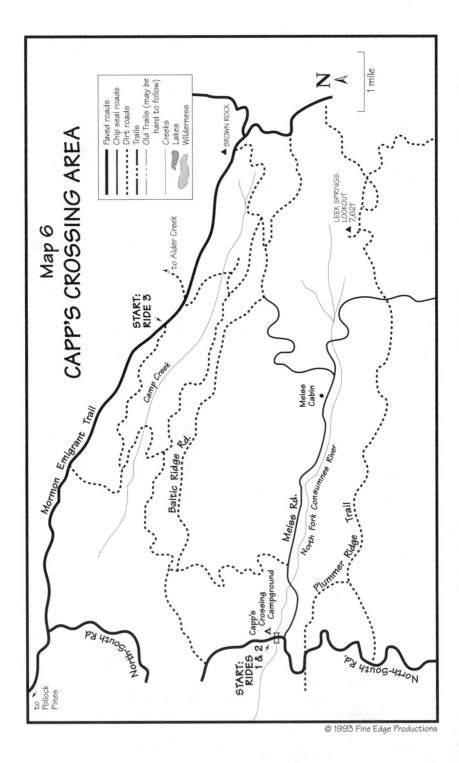

Map 6
CAPP'S CROSSING AREA

Mormon Emigrant Trail

to Alder Creek

BROWN ROCK

START: RIDE 3

Camp Creek

Baltic Ridge Rd.

LEEK SPRINGS LOOKOUT 7,621'

Meiss Cabin

Meiss Rd.

North Fork Consumnes River

Plummer Ridge Trail

North-South Rd.

to Pollock Pines

Capp's Crossing Campground

START: RIDES 1 & 2

North-South Rd.

Paved roads
Chip seal roads
Dirt roads
Trails
Old Trails (may be hard to follow)
Creeks
Lakes
Wilderness

N

1 mile

© 1993 Fine Edge Productions

The Ride: Ride up North-South Road a quarter mile, take the first road to the left, the Meiss Road. This road is paved, but it is still an enjoyable ride along the North Fork of the Consumnes River. The first road to the left is the Voss Cabin Road. This is the road you will come down if you ride the whole ride. (Camp Creek 11 miles, another dirt road worth exploring!) 4.5 miles out, you arrive at the Meiss Cabin site. Worth a stop to do a bit of exploring as judging by the tilt of these old cabins they won't be standing much longer. 0.5 mile later turn left at the sign that says *Baltic Ridge 4 miles.* The first mile is the steepest! After that it just continues to climb 1,000+ feet in 4 miles. 4 miles later—You're at the top and the end of the chip sealed road. Straight ahead goes up Baltic Ridge to Mormon Emigrant Trail. Turn left down the Baltic Ridge Road.

All along the ridge, there are roads that may be worth exploring. To stay on this ride, follow the ridge top. You ride through short ups and mostly downs, through a fuel break, then an old jeep road with lots of obstacles. After 6.1 miles, the road dead-ends into the Voss Cabin Road. Turn left (downhill). To the right is Camp Creek, 8 miles. 3 miles: Turn right on the paved road. You are back where you started. Continue out to North-South Road, turn right and head back to Capps Crossing for a swim.

Ride 2 The Ridge Ride

Mileage: 28 miles.
Topo Maps: 7.5 min. Stump Springs, Leek Springs Hill and Peddler Hill.
Water: Carry more than you think you will need! No water for 12 miles of climbing.
Level of Difficulty: Advanced or expert—those strong enough to ride 5 to 7 hours!
Elevation: 5,180'–7,621'.
Season: June through October. A good way to find out if this will be rideable is to ask if Mormon Emigrant Trail is open to Highway 88. Once the road is open and the snow has melted enough you should be able to negotiate the snow banks.

The Ride (from Capps Crossing): Continue out North-South Road to the top of the hill. Go past the road heading west towards Grizzly Flats. After 1.5 miles of pavement, turn left on Plummer Ridge Trail. Stay on the main road and follow all the signs marked Plummer Ridge Trail or Leek Springs Lookout. 8 miles later you reach a paved road (left to Buckskin Joe Springs), go across it and ride up the 4-wheel drive road. Here is where the climb begins! In the summers we've been sending riders out this way, I don't know of any who have made it from here to Leek Springs Lookout without putting a foot down once or twice!

Just when you think the up is over, you'll go down and have to climb back up again. Turn left at the Leek Springs Lookout sign for the final ascent to the lookout, elevation 7,621'. Have lunch then climb the tower and ask the lookout to show you where Capps Crossing is. You have travelled 12 miles. After resting, go down the hill (past the road you pedalled up) until you reach the paved road, Mormon Emigrant Trail, turn left. Stay on the pavement until you see a cattleguard (1 mile). Turn left on the dirt road just before the cattleguard. Follow the main road, the road farthest to the left.

Stay on the main road (we'll call this Upper Baltic Ridge Road), go around the cattleguard and continue the descent. 2.5 miles, turn left following the sign to Capps Crossing. This road is fast and simple, so one mile farther, take the road to the right (nearly straight ahead). The road to the left is paved all the way back to Capps Crossing. If you are tired, this is the easy way home! You are now on the "Meiss Cabin/Baltic Ridge Ride." Continue out the ridge staying on the main road following the ridge top. You ride through short ups and downs, through a fuel break then back on the old jeep road with lots of obstacles. After 6.1 miles the road dead-ends into the Voss Cabin Road. Turn left, downhill. 3 miles later turn right on the paved road (Meiss Road). Turn right on the North-South Road for a short downhill to the car.

Ride 3   Camp Creek Loop

Topo Maps: 7.5 min. Leek Springs Hill. Start: T10N, 15E, section 33.
Mileage: 8.7 miles.
Elevation: 5,600–6,200'.
Water: Usually water in Camp Creek until late August. Filter or treat all water.
Level of Difficulty: Easy ride. Good one for morning ride, afternoon swim. Or add this ride onto one of the Capps Crossing rides for more mileage.
Camping: Dispersed camping is allowed on Forest Service land with a campfire permit. Be sure to check for any fire restrictions. The closest campground is Capps Crossing. In fact, you can ride this loop from Capps Crossing if you are looking for a longer ride.
Nearest Services: 21 miles in Pollock Pines

The Drive: From Placerville, take U.S. 50 east to Pollock Pines. Take the second offramp, Sly Park Road, turn right (south) on Sly Park Road. Continue 4.5 miles. Just past the lake turn left on Mormon Emigrant Trail. Reset your odometer because the next turn is hard to find. 16.2 miles out the Mormon Emigrant Trail you will find a road going south called Upper Pilliken (no sign). Park by the intersection, or if you want to end at a good swimming spot drive down Upper Pilliken, turn left at the intersection (2 miles). Drive until you see some large rocks on the right hand side. Park here, the swimming hole is just down the hill from the rocks.

The Ride: From Mormon Emigrant Trail, continue up Mormon Emigrant Trail 0.3 mile, turn right on the first road. After 1 mile a road enters from the left; continue on the main road which turns to chip seal for a short section. Cross Camp Creek and turn right at the next intersection. Ride a short distance. 0.1 mile go left uphill. (Road straight ahead is a short 1 mile road along the creek that ends up the same place you are heading.) After a bit of climbing and winding around on the ridge for about 2 miles, turn right at the intersection continuing downhill. (Left takes you to the top of the ridge then down to Capps Crossing Campground.) Ride downhill across Camp Creek, then the road continues along the creek; look for big rocks to the left. Just behind the rocks, down on the creek, is a swimming hole. If you parked here your ride is done. If not, continue on and turn right. Here is where you pay for all the fun you had going downhill. It's 2 miles uphill to Mormon Emigrant Trail. The uphill is not bad, though many cyclists prefer to start at the creek and ride up first.

ALDER CREEK AREA *Map 7*

The Drive: From Pollock Pines take Sly Park Road 4.5 miles to Jenkinson Lake and turn left on Mormon Emigrant Trail. Continue 16.6 miles to Alder Creek Road. Turn left (north), continue on for 3 miles to a bridge that crosses Alder Creek. The rides on Map 7 start here, T10N, R15E, section 27. Parking is usually available on either side of the bridge.
Campgrounds: Closest campgrounds are Sly Park 22 miles, Capps Crossing (see Map 6 this chapter), or Silverfork Campground on Silverfork Road. Undeveloped campsites are located all along Alder Creek. Be advised that there is a lot of private land along Alder Creek and you may not camp on the private land!
Nearest Services: Pollock Pines, 26 miles.

Ride 1   Alder Ridge Lookout Loop

Mileage: 15 miles.
Maps: 7.5 min. Leek Springs Hill; 15 min. Leek Springs Hill.
Water: Carry all the water you think you'll need (plus more!) There are no water stops until you are almost back to your car!
Level of Difficulty: Intermediate, or beginners looking for a challenge.
Elevation: 5,300'–6,192'.

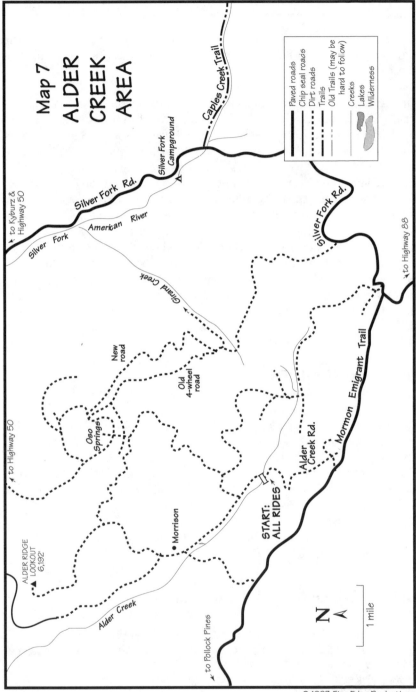

Map 7
ALDER
CREEK
AREA

Caples Creek Trail

to Kyburz &
Highway 50

Silver Fork Rd.

Silver Fork
Campground

Silver Fork

American River

Grand Creek

New
road

Old 4-wheel
road

Oso
Springs

Silver Fork Rd.

to Highway 88

to Highway 50

Morrison

Alder
Creek Rd.

Mormon Emigrant Trail

START:
ALL RIDES

ALDER RIDGE
LOOKOUT
6,192'

Alder Creek

to Pollock Pines

N

1 mile

Paved roads
Chip seal roads
Dirt roads
Trails
Old Trails (may be
hard to follow)
Creeks
Lakes
Wilderness

© 1993 Fine Edge Productions

The Ride: Cross the bridge and continue 0.7 mile out Alder Creek Road. Take the first right uphill marked *Oso Springs.* 1 mile: Turn left at the next intersection following the sign to Oso Springs. 5 miles: Stay on the main road through some fast downhills and more uphills. At the next intersection, turn left following the signs to *Alder Ridge Lookout* (2 miles to the top). 0.5 mile later take the next road to the right (follow the sign to Alder Ridge). Ride across the ridge and up to the lookout. Elevation 6,192'. Take a break, then climb to the top of the lookout tower. The tower is small, so if you have a group, don't all go up at once. Ride back down the hill and turn right when you reach the main road again. Enjoy the fast downhills ending with a creek crossing. You have now returned to the Alder Creek Road. Continue on past Morrisons (cabins, range cattle, etc.) and back to your car. If you feel like swimming, ride or drive downstream to some great swimming pools!

Ride 2   Alder/Oso Springs Loop

Mileage: Oso Loop from the bridge—9.7 miles. This loop can be added to Ride 1 or 3 for extra mileage.
Level of Difficulty: Easy to intermediate

The Ride: Cross the bridge and continue out Alder Creek Road. Take the first right uphill, 0.7 mile, at the sign *Oso Springs.* 1 mile: Turn left at the next intersection following the sign to *Oso Springs [left].* The road to the right is signed *Dead-end Road* (but it's not!). 3.5 miles: Turn right up the short, steep uphill (if you missed this right turn, the next one goes to the same place). You come to an intersection (west goes to Alder Ridge Lookout, east goes to Silverfork Road). Go straight ahead for the Oso Loop. At the next intersection, go left towards Highway 50. (Straight takes you to Oso Springs.) Continue down the road towards Highway 50, turn right on the first major right marked 11A. In a short quarter mile you cross one creek drainage (Beanville Creek—it may be dry).

Take the next right uphill. (If you cross Beanville Creek for a second time right away, go back, you missed the turn—the road that continues straight ahead is fun to ride, but it dead-ends in 1.5 miles.) Continue along the side of the creek. Part of the road has become the creek bed and the road is completely washed out for a short distance, but the road is good on the other side. Go around the corner and keep looking for a meadow on the left side. If it's still green, get off your bike and look at Beanville Meadow. If it happens to be late July or early August, the

Kamikaze singletrack

California coneflowers (*Rudebeckia californica*) should be in bloom. These are rare yellow daisy-like flowers with large cone centers.

After looking for flowers, continue on through an open area then up a short hill. If you are continuing on the Alder Loop go left when you reach the top of the hill. If you are riding the Oso Loop or want to go to Alder Ridge Lookout, go right and you will come back to the Oso Springs. Follow your tracks back down to the bridge or follow the signs to Alder Ridge Lookout and read the directions for Ride 1.

Ride 3   Alder Ridge/Ridge Ride

Topo Maps: 7.5 min. Leek Springs Hill; Tragedy Springs.
Mileage: 26 miles.
Water: Oso Springs and several creeks. Treat or filter all water.
Elevation: 5,300–6,540'.
Seasons: Mid-May through October.
Level of Difficulty: Intermediate riders looking for a 5- to 7-hour ride.

The Ride: Follow Ride 2 directions to Alder Ridge/Silverfork Road sign. There are two different roads you can ride to complete this ride. For simplicity they are described as Options 1 and 2. *Option 1* is an old 4-wheel drive road, rocky and steep. This is the road that is shown on the Eldorado National Forest Map as the Alder Ridge 4-wheel drive road. Choose Option 1 if you like rough, rocky rides! *Option 2* is a newer, wider, smooth dirt road that contours around on the northeast side of Alder Ridge. At the present time this road is not on any of the Forest Service maps or USGS maps available to the public. Choose Option 2 if you prefer wider, smoother dirt roads. Now that you have made your decision, follow Option 1 or 2, they join back together approximately 3 miles later.

Option 1: The first road to the right (at the Alder Ridge lookout sign) goes up a steep hill through a burn (clear cut area). When you reach the top, go right down the ridge following the old 4-wheel drive road shown on all the maps. This is the rougher, more challenging option.

Option 2: Go straight at the Alder Ridge/Silverfork sign towards Oso Springs. Take the next right and you come to a new ridge road not yet shown on any maps. **Warning:** Stay on the main road that contours up and down the ridge! Remember all roads to the left drop quickly from 6,500' to 5,200' and you have to regain the elevation eventually!

Option 1 and 2 join together just before they cross Girard Creek. Continue on straight ahead past the sign that says *Hell's Delight 3 miles,*

Silverfork Road 1 mile. One mile later turn right on the paved road (Silverfork Road). Go uphill 1.5 miles on the pavement, over the cattleguard, around the turn, then take the first dirt road to the right (downhill). The road forks immediately; continue straight ahead. You arrive at a meadow restoration project (small 4' X 4' posts placed around the edge of the meadow to keep 4-wheel drivers out of the mud). Turn right and cross Upper Alder Creek and continue on the main road.

At the Y intersection go right, uphill, for the last climb that goes around the ridge, then get ready for some fast, screaming downhill to the sign *Dead-end Road /Oso Springs.* (You just rode down the dead-end road!) Turn left, then left again, following your tracks back to the car.

3 HIGHWAY 50/ AMERICAN RIVER CANYON

Pony Express Historical Trail/Old Blair Bridge Loop;
Round Tent Canyon Loop; Pacific House to Kyburz Loop;
Strawberry Canyon Out and Back; Strawberry to
Highway 88; Strawberry Loop; Strawberry Creek Loop;
Barrett Lake; Wrights Lake to Pearl Lake

PEAVINE RIDGE AREA   *Map 8*

The Drive: To get to the trailhead, drive east on U.S. 50, 8 miles past Pollock Pines. Turn left on Ice House Road. Half a mile along (where the main road swings sharply to the right), go straight ahead on Forest Road 35, the White Meadow Road. For longer rides you could also park here, but to ride the first short loop, continue driving 1.2 miles to a turnout on the left side of the road in the middle of a sharp right turn. Park here. Note: If you have ridden in this area over the years, note that the old trailhead at Pacific House is no longer used because the Blair Bridge across the American River was destroyed.

Nearest Services: Ice House Resort, with a small store, restaurant, gas station and bar, is located 9 miles up Ice House Road. Major services are available in Pollock Pines, 8 miles west on U.S. 50.

Camping: Several USFS campgrounds are located up Ice House Road (see Chapter 4, Crystal Basin Area). If you are riding before Memorial Day or after Labor Day—the best times here—the closest campground still open is at Sly Park, to the west on U.S. 50 in Pollock Pines (see Chapter 2, Pollock Pines/Iron Mountain Road Area).

Seasons: The majority of riding on Peavine Ridge is on south facing slopes, which means it drys out quickly, and is some of the warmest early and late season riding. *This area is extremely hot in the middle of the summer.* The best time to ride is March through June and September through November, unless you are one who enjoys the heat!

The following rides are just suggestions of what is possible from Forest Road 35, the White Meadow Road. Several roads travel through private land, most belonging to Michigan-California Lumber Co. Some of these roads are open because they travel in and out of U.S. Forest Service land; others may be closed due to logging activities. Much of the land along the White Meadow Road (Forest Road 35) is now owned by private homeowners. *Respect all private land signs by staying on the roads and travelling on through.*

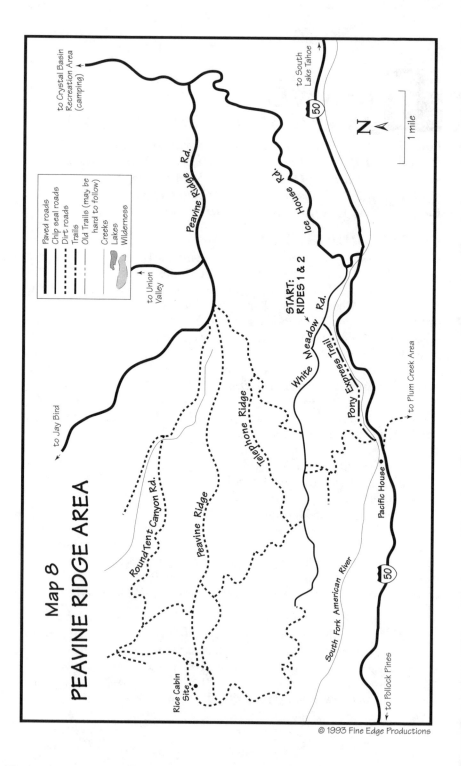

Map 8
PEAVINE RIDGE AREA

to Crystal Basin Recreation Area (camping)

to Union Valley

to Jay Bird

to South Lake Tahoe

50

N

1 mile

Paved roads
Chip seal roads
Dirt roads
Trails
Old Trails (may be hard to follow)
Creeks
Lakes
Wilderness

Peavine Ridge Rd.

Ice House Rd.

START: RIDES 1 & 2

White Meadow Rd.

Pony Express Trail

to Plum Creek Area

RoundTent Canyon Rd.

Telephone Ridge

Peavine Ridge

Rice Cabin Site

South Fork American River

Pacific House

50

to Pollock Pines

© 1993 Fine Edge Productions

Ride 1   Pony Express Historical Trail/ Old Blair Bridge Loop

Topo Maps: 7.5 min. Pollock Pines and Riverton. Start: T11N, R14E, section 19.
Elevation: 3,100'–3,820'.
Mileage: 9.2 miles.
Level of Difficulty: Short, intermediate level loop with a fun 2-mile downhill section and half a mile of technical single track.
Water: Definitely available at the 5.7 mile spot at the American River, but you will have to hike to get to it. Other small streams usually have water, too. Filter or treat all water taken from streams.

The Ride: Continue out Forest Road 35 on your bike. It goes up right away with not much of a chance to warm up! At 1.9 miles, continue on straight ahead on the paved road past a sign to White Meadows Camp (in the direction of Blairs Mill Site). At 3.0 miles, stay to the left on the main road (right reads "Peavine Road").

At nearly 3.5 miles turn left (green sign reads "Peavine Ridge Rd") and prepare for a fast 2-mile downhill run! (If you missed this turn, 3.6 miles out you will ride past Whale Rock, a large boulder painted to look like the head of a whale. Look to your left and you will see another road going down into the river canyon. Go left; this spur soon ties into the main road. *Warning:* Watch out for the deep ruts at the beginning and end of the spur road!)

5.3 miles: When you ride through a sharp right turn, look to your left for the Pony Express Trail, which you will ride to complete the loop. But continue on past it if you want to get a look at the American River, go for a swim and see where the old bridge used to cross. At 5.7 miles, the road ends abruptly at a large water bar. Leave your bikes and walk to the edge of the canyon. If you want to swim or wade, the best route down is to follow the creek drainage off to the left. As you look across the river, you can see the road we used to ride down. There is a possibility that someday a foot bridge may cross the river. This would be nice, but it's probably several years away. *Warning:* The river is deep and swift at this location, usually all summer long, so do not plan your trip thinking you will be able to ford the river at this spot! When you are done enjoying the river, ride back up to Pony Express Trail.

After riding 6.0 miles from your starting point, you turn right and head out on the remnants of the Pony Express Trail, used by Pony Express riders in the 1800s to deliver the mail. This is a challenging stretch of single track that is worth attempting, but be careful of the washouts!

Poised for the downhill

Take time to look at the old rock wall built into the hillside to form the trail. Don't worry if you have trouble here; this is a short section you can walk if you need to. Soon the trail widens out into an old road.

At 6.8 miles, a newer, wider road crosses the road you are on. Turn right and ride down a short, steep section. Keep right again, staying on the main road. Soon you reach a take-down cattle fence. Be sure to leave it as you found it, open or closed. This is a tough fence to take down, so if you have someone with you, crawl through the fence and pass your bikes over the top. Continue on, watching for cows if the gate was closed. From here the road rolls along, climbing and descending over and over as you travel along the river canyon.

When the dirt road ends at 9.0 miles, you have reached Forest Road 35. Turn left and ride the final 0.2 mile back to your car. (If you started from Ice House Road, turn right and you have 1.2 miles more to go.)

Ride 2   Round Tent Canyon Loop

Topo Maps: 7.5 min. Pollock Pines and Riverton. Start: T11N, R14E, section 19. Elevation: 3,500'–4,914'.
Mileage: 27 miles total.
Level of Difficulty: Intermediate to advanced ride, not extremely technical, but you gain and lose elevation several times, so it requires riders with endurance.
Water: Usually available in Round Tent Canyon, but carry extra just in case you turn around before you get that far.

The Ride: Follow the driving directions in Ride 1 and park at the turnout. Continue on out Forest Road 35, White Meadow Road. Most of the first section is paved or chipped sealed, but it is a good warm-up before the steeper dirt section begins. At 3.6 miles, look off to your right and you should see Whale Rock. Continue on.

At 4.0 miles, turn right at the intersection, following the sign to Telephone Ridge. Sign: Spring V*alley [left]; Rice Cabin [left]; Telephone Ridge [right]; Peavine Ridge [right]; McManus [right].* 1.2 miles: Turn right onto the Telephone Ridge Road and travel 0.6 mile. Stay on the main road which turns right. Several roads cross the Telephone Ridge Road, just remember the idea is to stay up on Telephone Ridge. If you drop off to the north (left) you will have to climb back out again.

After about 0.5 mile, the road falls apart for about 1.4 miles. It is technical riding on a cobbled lava cap on a hot treeless slope. It is all rideable, but you may choose to walk certain short, steep sections. When you reach the end of the cobbles, turn left on the top of the ridge. The road follows the fence line then forks 0.2 miles. Turn right through the take-down gate (or opening in the fence line). The ride now takes you out on the ridge looking out to the east. The prominent peak straight east is Pyramid Peak. Off to the southeast are the rugged mountains of Carson Pass. After 1.7 miles, you are at the top of Peavine Ridge, elevation 4,914'. This is a four-way intersection, with *lots* of signs. Get out your map to figure it all out. The dirt road to your left (east) is Peavine Ridge Road. The paved road to your right goes to Ice House Road (this is also Peavine Ridge Road). The paved road to the left goes to Jay Bird Power House and Reservoir.

Go left on the paved road for 0.2 mile, turn left on Round Tent Canyon Road. Sign says *Road Closed 3 miles.* 1.1 mile farther, watch out for a gate while you are flying downhill! Some times it's open, and other times it's closed. 0.7 miles along, go left toward Round Tent Creek (road to the right eventually dead-ends overlooking Camino Reservoir). If you need water, this is the place to stop. Be sure to filter or treat all your water! 4 miles later you will be treated to an overlook of Camino Reservoir. 0.8 mile: when you see the microwave station on the point of the ridge, look to your left for a road that goes straight uphill. Go up this road to the top of the hill. (The road straight ahead dead-ends.)

After you have reached the top, you drop off through a clear cut in the forest. Without all the trees, you are treated to a great view of the Crystal Range and the highest peak, Pyramid Peak. You are now crossing through private land, with a maze of roads. Continue downhill on the main road. 0.6 mile at the bottom of a downhill, turn right (just past K tag T11N, R13E, center section 8). Follow the signs to Rice Cabin. 0.8 mile, turn right at the sign that says: *Soldier Creek [left]; Indian Hattes [right]*. Go toward Indian Hattes. At 0.1 mile, you come to an intersection. You can go straight or go right towards Rice Cabin. If you go right out Rice Ridge Road, take the next left just before the road drops off downhill (dead-end). 0.6 mile on the loop, you arrive at the Rice Cabin site. Unfortunately, compared to many old homesteads, there's not much left to see.

Continue straight ahead to the sign 1.2 miles: *Soldier Creek, Spring Valley [left]*. Turn left at this intersection. 0.9 mile later: After a downhill, turn right. (I know it feels like you should go left here, but trust the sign, it is a dead-end!) The road makes an immediate, wide left turn to get you headed east. Continue winding in and out of canyon after canyon. Stay on the main road that changes from gravel to dirt. 4.7 miles later you are back to the first Telephone Ridge sign. Continue straight ahead.

Another 0.5 mile farther, when you reach Whale Rock, you can either continue on Forest Road 35 back to your car or, to make your day's run into an expert-level ride, turn right and follow the directions in Ride 1 down into the canyon to the American River.

Ride 3   Pacific House to Kyburz Loop   *Map* **9**

Topo Maps: 7.5 min. Riverton, Stump Springs, Leek Spring Hill and Kyburz.
Elevation: 3,100'–5,200'.
Mileage: 27 miles +.
Level of Difficulty: A good ride for early in the season to build up your distance riding skills. The ride is over 27 miles, with options to go even farther. Good climbs mix in with good downhills and even a couple of short trail options. This ride is for strong intermediates or better.
Water: Several small streams usually have water. Filter or treat all water taken from these creeks.

The Drive: This ride used to be done as a loop from Pacific House, but since the bridge across the American River was removed it now takes two cars to do the whole ride. Leave one car at the intersection of Ice House Road and Forest Road 35 (see Ride 1). Drive the other car to the start of the ride at Pacific House, 4.5 miles east of Pollock Pines on U.S. 50.

The Ride: The first task is to cross Highway 50, so watch out for the traffic! Turn left on Hazel Valley Road, which curves to the right, then climbs the ridge in front of you. Ride across the bridge over the P.G.& E. ditch (cement walled stream) and continue on up the hill (0.8 mile). In a short distance (0.1), you arrive at a sign: *Plum Creek Road [left]; Park Creek Road [right].* Go left following the sign to Plum Creek. (Either way works here, if you go right toward Park Creek, turn left when you reach the next road.) 0.8 mile later: Turn left on Plum Creek Road, climb a bit more, then enjoy the gradual up and down fast paced spinning to Plum Creek. 5.3 miles: Cross Plum Creek and continue straight ahead uphill. (The road to the right goes to Upper Plum Creek.) The road you are on is known by the locals as "Highway to Heaven." This used to be a tough climb up a deeply rutted road, but during the summer of 1989 it was chipped sealed. It is still a good long 1,000-foot climb, but the smoother road conditions make it much easier. Just when you think you're all through, the road turns and goes up some more. Once on top, there's a flat section, then a downhill across Mill Creek. (3 miles from Plum Creek to Mill Creek.) Don't count on Mill Creek for water late in the summer.

At the four-way intersection, take the middle road (the road to the right is the route for the "Mountain Mania" mountain bike race). The next 2

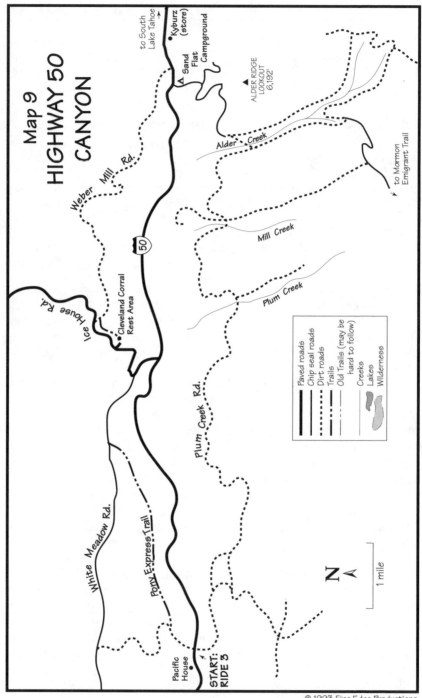

Map 9
HIGHWAY 50 CANYON

to South Lake Tahoe →
Kyburz (store)
Sand Flat
Campground
ALDER RIDGE LOOKOUT 6,192'
Alder Creek
to Mormon Emigrant Trail
Weber Mill Rd.
50
Mill Creek
Plum Creek
Ice House Rd.
Cleveland Corral Rest Area
Plum Creek Rd.
White Meadow Rd.
Pony Express Trail
Pacific House
START: RIDE 3

Paved roads
Chip seal roads
Dirt roads
Trails
Old Trails (may be hard to follow)
Creeks
Lakes
Wilderness

N
1 mile

© 1993 Fine Edge Productions

miles can be the hottest of the ride. This ride goes through the Pilliken Fire area, which burned in 1973. The trees are now taller than the brush, but it will be a few years before they give riders much shade. 2.1 miles: The climbing is done for a while. Down in the canyon below is Highway 50. The ridge to the east is Alder Ridge. Look carefully at the high point that still has trees on it, and you should be able to spot the lookout tower. As you round the corner to the Alder Creek drainage, you'll get a glimpse at just how huge and devastating this fire was! 1.1 miles later: Look for a road to the left that drops off down to Alder Creek. Just opposite the turn is a stump with two wooden signs, one sign has "2" on it and the other one a "6." The road across the canyon on Alder Ridge (you see that is just above level with you) is now your goal. This 0.7-mile shortcut saves you about 7 miles of riding up the drainage to Duffy's Crossing. Where the shortcut crosses Alder Creek there is a wonderful swimming pool if anyone is ready for a swim.

When you reach the other road, turn left. The road eventually turns to chip seal, then it's a fast 3.2 miles downhill to Highway 50. If you brought lunch, this is a good spot to rest and get water. If you need a snack, the Silverfork Store is located about a half mile east on Highway 50 (turn right). 0.2 mile: Go east on Highway 50 and turn left (north) onto Weber Mill Road (just over 17 miles to this point). Now you have to regain some of the altitude you lost in the last downhill.

After 7.5 miles Weber Mill Road turns right and 0.2 mile later it ties into a major paved road—Ice House Road. Turn left then ride downhill to Cleveland Corral. Or, look straight ahead in the last turn and follow the old road over the underground lines. This road turns into a trail that also leads to Cleveland Corral Picnic Area. Restrooms and cold water! Continue downhill on Ice House Road into the big left turn. Turn right in the middle of the turn onto White Meadow Road and you should see your car. If you are still ready to ride more, see Ride 1 to add on an 11-mile loop down to where the old Blair Bridge used to be.

STRAWBERRY CANYON   *Map 10*

Topo Maps: 7.5 min. Pyramid Peak, Echo Lake, Caples Lake, Tragedy Springs.15 min. Fallen Leak Lake, Silver Lake. Ride starts: T11NR, 17E, section 19.
Level of Difficulty: This area is best suited to very strong riders, especially rides 2 and 3.
Seasons: Mid-June through October.

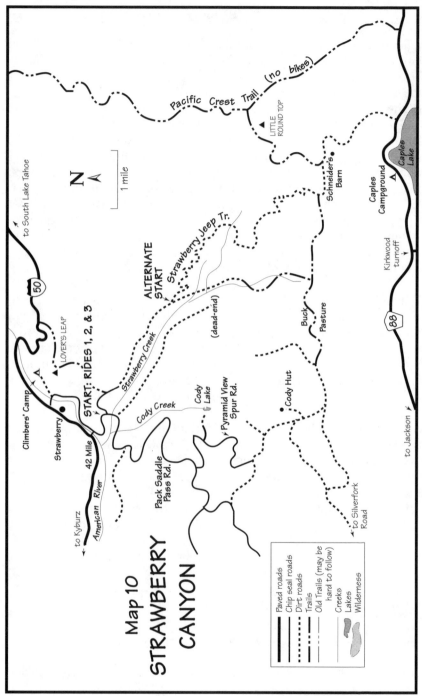

Map 10
STRAWBERRY CANYON

Pacific Crest Trail (no bikes)

LITTLE ROUND TOP

to South Lake Tahoe

N

1 mile

Caples Lake

Schneider's Barn

Caples Campground

Kirkwood turnoff

50

Strawberry Jeep Tr.

ALTERNATE START

88

LOVER'S LEAP

START: RIDES 1, 2, & 3

Strawberry Creek

(dead-end)

Buck Pasture

Climbers' Camp

Strawberry

42 Mile

Cody Creek

Cody Lake

Pyramid View Spur Rd.

Cody Hut

to Kyburz

American River

Pack Saddle Pass Rd.

to Silverfork Road

to Jackson

Paved roads
Chip seal roads
Dirt roads
Trails
Old Trails (may be hard to follow)
Creeks
Lakes
Wilderness

© 1993 Fine Edge Productions

The Drive: Take U.S. 50 east toward South Lake Tahoe to 42 mile picnic area, located on the right just before you reach the big meadow at Strawberry. Look for a large Eldorado National Forest sign that reads *Picnic Ground* and *42 mile* under it. Turn right into the picnic area, then drive across the bridge and turn right again. 0.6 mile from the Highway turn left following the signs to Strawberry Canyon. The sign says *Strawberry 4x4 Rd.* You can park here or continue 2.6 miles where the jeep road takes off. It's nice to start from this intersection, as it gives you a chance to warm up with a gradual climb, before starting in on the Strawberry Canyon Jeep Trail which starts off quite steep.

About the Area: This is a good area to remember if you are a rock climber or are travelling with climbers. Just up Highway 50, about a half mile farther, is the famous climbing spot called Lover's Leap. After you ride, be sure to drive over to the base, then hike or bike out to take a look. This area has grown in popularity, so there are usually several groups of climbers on their way up to the top. If you are intrigued by the Leap, and are not a climber, there are two hiking trails to the top. You ride by one of them if you do the Strawberry Canyon Jeep Trail Ride, and the other easier hike is from Camp Sacramento. *Both trails receive heavy hiker use and are not suited for mountain bikes. Please leave your bikes back at the car!*

Camping: Lodging is available at Strawberry Lodge. There is a U.S. Forest Service climber campground located at the base of Lover's Leap. It is usually very crowded on weekends, whenever the weather is good. Next closest campgrounds are at Sand Flat, 10 miles west on Highway 50, Wrights Lake, north of Kyburz on Wrights Lake Road and China Flat, south of Kyburz on Silverfork Road.

Nearest Services: Store, gas station, restaurant, bar and lodging at Strawberry.

Ride 1   Strawberry Canyon Out and Back

Ride, or drive the 2.6 miles back to the trailhead on your left, marked Strawberry Canyon Jeep Trail. (You pass the hiking trail to the top of Lover's Leap on your left in a half mile.) Don't panic! The trail is not all as steep and torn up as this first hill. Usually the jeepers have the first hill so torn up that most people will have to walk. Starting from the Strawberry side, the jeep trail climbs from 6,360' to 8,600' in about 7 miles (5,800', if you start from Highway 50). This means you climb over 2,000 feet, with some of the pitches quite steep and loose, but not too long, and the rest of it is just good, steady climbing. Your surroundings change from dense white fir, cedar and pine forest, to red fir, then at higher elevation hemlocks, western white pines and juniper trees. Try to pay attention to the turns and rough spots on your way up, so you can enjoy the FAST descent on the way down. When you reach the top, retrace your tracks the way you came.

Ride 2   Strawberry to Highway 88

Follow Ride 1 to the top of the ridge. Continue ahead on the main road, which turns east, then the descent begins down to Schneider's Barn and Highway 88. The views from the road are some of the best and the wildflowers can be waist deep from mid-July to early August. Be sure to carry a topo map, so you can pick out Thimble Peak (Kirkwood Ski Area), Round Top and Elephant's Back at Carson Pass. 1.5 miles in the meadow on the right, you'll see Schneider's Barn —an old cow camp. Be careful through here, as cows may be grazing right across the road. If you see cows, be on the lookout for take-down fences that may be up across the road. *Be sure to leave the gates as you found them!* 1.5 miles—The ride ends at Highway 88. If you are in need of refreshments, turn right on Highway 88, cross the dam and you arrive at Caples Lake Resort, with a small store, restaurant and cabins for rent.

Those who are hardy can leave Strawberry early, have lunch at Caples, then ride back to Strawberry in the afternoon. Total mileage out and back is only 24 miles, but you gain over 3,000' for the day's ride. Note: The easy way to do this ride is to be dropped off at Caples Maintenance Station on Highway 88, ride up the Caples side and down the Strawberry side.

Ride 3   Strawberry Loop

Follow Ride 1 to the top of the ridge. Don't do this one without topo and USFS maps, and your compass, so you can see all your options! Turn right (west) through the boulders on a two wheel trail to Buck Pasture. It is technical and fun at first, but after you leave Buck Pasture, the trail climbs out on a south facing slope. You will find yourself in a hot, dry spot pushing your bike through decomposed granite (sand). Riding in this direction is only for those looking for a real adventure!

The 2-wheel trail turns into a jeep trail. (The first road to the right goes out on Strawberry Ridge and dead-ends.) Continue straight ahead. The next fork goes to the left toward Hay Flat, then on downhill to Silverfork Road. Continue straight. The road turns and you ride along the ridge above Cody Meadows. Continue straight ahead and in 1 mile two roads to the left go downhill to N-Flat, then eventually down to Silverfork Road. The road to the right is a short half mile down to an old cow herder's cabin, which is now used in the winter as the Cody Ski Hut. Continue

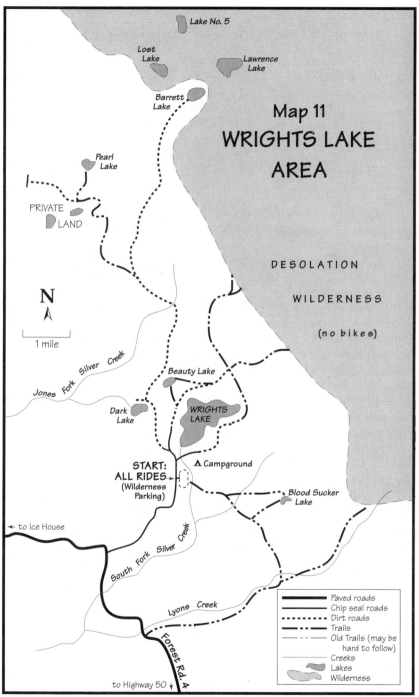

Lake No. 5

Lost
Lake

Lawrence
Lake

Barrett
Lake

Map 11
WRIGHTS LAKE
AREA

Pearl
Lake

PRIVATE
LAND

D E S O L A T I O N

W I L D E R N E S S

(no bikes)

N
∧

1 mile

Jones Fork Silver Creek

Beauty Lake

Dark
Lake

WRIGHTS
LAKE

START:
ALL RIDES
(Wilderness
Parking)

▲ Campground

Blood Sucker
Lake

← to Ice House

South Fork Silver Creek

Lyons Creek

Forest Rd. 4

to Highway 50 ↓

▬▬▬	Paved roads
——	Chip seal roads
••••••	Dirt roads
▬ ▬ ▬	Trails
– · – · –	Old Trails (may be hard to follow)
——	Creeks
🌫	Lakes
	Wilderness

© 1993 Fine Edge Productions

straight ahead, as the road starts to climb again.

In 0.8 mile you reach the top. The road to the right goes out to Cody overlook, where you get a great view of Cody Lake and Pyramid Peak. Continue straight ahead, as the road winds around the ridge, then ties into Pyramid View Spur, a better road. The riding is fast and easy from here. Continue down, turn right on Pack Saddle Pass Road which takes you back down to the first intersection that goes to Strawberry Canyon, then on to Highway 50 and 42 Mile Picnic Area. *Note:* If you choose this route, be sure to carry lots of water and food, as it is definitely an all day adventure! Late in the season, you may not find water until you get to Cody Meadows, and then the meadow may be full of cows.

Ride 4   Strawberry Creek Loop

Mileage: 14 miles.
Level of Difficulty: Advanced, with a steep climb and a technical downhill.
Caution: Be on the lookout for hikers and horseback riders.

Follow Ride 1 to the top of the ridge. 7 miles: Turn right (west) on the 2-wheel drive trail to Buck Pasture. The trail is rough and rocky at first, then enters a forested area. After about 1.5 miles (8.5 miles total), look to your right (north) for a singletrack trail heading back into Strawberry Canyon. *Warning:* This is a steep, technical downhill for advanced riders only. After a mile, the trail ends at a jeep road, which crosses the creek and takes you to a gate that is usually closed. Go around the gate and you are back on the road you started on, which takes you back to your vehicle.

WRIGHTS LAKE AREA   *Map 11*

The Drive: Go east on U.S. 50 through the town of Kyburz. Five miles east of Kyburz look for a sign that points the way to Wrights Lake. Turn left here and drive 8 miles to the campground. This is a great campground for spending a couple of days—find a campsite early because this is one of the few Forest Service Campgrounds that people can make reservations for. (Call the USFS Information Center at 916-644-6048 for reservations.) If it is a busy weekend, you should park at the Wilderness Parking Lot you'll see on the right. Limited parking is available at the trailhead. The Wrights Lake area is also accessible from the Ice House Road in the Crystal Basin Area. Hiking trails, roads and two wheel drive roads radiate all around Wrights Lake. This is a nice place to explore in August when the dust gets bad down below. Some cyclists begin their ride just off of U.S. 50 and make a day of riding to Wrights Lake (just over 8 miles), exploring a while, and then riding back down to U.S. 50. The elevation gain from the highway to the lake is just over 1,500 feet,

Wrights Lake

and with exploration, the total mileage usually is 20 miles or more.

Caution: There is a horse staging area at the lake which means you must be a safe rider at all times. So far, mountain bikes have a free range on the trails and roads of Eldorado National Forest (with the exception of designated Wilderness Areas). *Please, help us keep it this way!*

Ride 1   Barrett Lake

Level of Difficulty: This ride following the "Barrett Lake Jeep Trail" is designed only for those who want a "rock-picking technical" ride and those who don't mind walking, as everyone walks a bit on this one! The nice part is it is only 12 miles round trip, so you could walk the whole thing if you had to! We took a marathon runner on this ride, who finally got so frustrated she hid her bike, and jogged in at the same pace as we were riding! Allow 4 to 5 hours to complete this ride if you are an "average" rider.

Topo maps: Start: 7.5 min. Pyramid Peak; Rockbound Valley. T12N, R16E, section 32.

Mileage: 12 miles.

Water: Lots if you have a filter.

Elevation: 6,900'–7,600'.

The Ride: From the Wilderness Parking area at Wrights Lake , follow the sign to Dark Lake. Ride 0.8 mile to the end of the "good" road at Dark Lake. Follow the jeep road that goes up immediately. The first hill is tricky but rideable if you find the right line. Stay on the Barrett Lake Jeep Road all the way to the lake. You ride through several creek crossings and two meadows. Be careful, they can be quite muddy through July—*No bikes alllowed in the Wilderness (all trails heading east). You can be ticketed for riding beyond the well-marked boundaries!*

Ride 2   Wrights Lake to Pearl Lake

Total Mileage: 10 miles.
Level of Difficulty: Intermediate or better.
Season: Mid-June through mid-October or the first good snow.

The Ride: This ride starts out the same as the Barrett Lake ride. After you cross the Jones Fork of Silver Creek, ride on to the first big meadow at 0.8 mile, called Mortimer Flat. Just as you reach the meadow, look uphill to the left, by a downed log, to find the trail to Pearl Lake. This trail is actually an old jeep road, so the width of the trail is good in a lot of places. The Pearl Lake trail is easy to follow, just stay on the main trail. The trail climbs up a hill, then follows the contour, then climbs up a rocky road section, then there's a fun downhill section. You can see a lake off to your left—*this is not Pearl Lake and it is all private land down below.* Reduce your speed, as the trail turns into road. Stay on the road, which is on private land, to the sign to Pearl Lake. After another 1.5 miles, turn right and follow the sandy road to Pearl Lake. Enjoy the solitude and the lake, then ride back out the way you came. *Caution:* The only other people we have seen in this area are horseback riders. Be prepared to see riders on the trail!

4 CRYSTAL BASIN AREA

Ice House Lakeshore; Ice House to Wrights Lake Out and Back; Big Hill Lookout; Bassi Out and Back; Two Peaks Hill Climb; Shadow Lake; Loon Lake Trail; The Slabs; Loon Lake Loop; McKinstry Lake Loop

This large recreation area is located 8 miles east of Pollock Pines on U.S. Highway 50. Just after you cross over the American River, take the immediate left on Ice House Road. There is a sign that read *Crystal Basin Recreation Area—Ice House Road.* Ice House Road is the main paved road running north/south through the area, and it takes you through the scene of the Cleveland Fire, which swept through here in 1992. Most of the rides in this section are located in areas untouched by the fire, so don't be discouraged by the drive—unlimited dirt riding for the adventurous types radiates from this road! The rides described in this section are relatively well-traveled, easy routes; they are only suggestions to get you started.

Several Forest Service Campgrounds are located in this area. Since many of them are on lakes, you can combine your biking with other recreation. Primitive camping is allowed on the National Forest Land, with a campfire permit. Be aware that there is a lot of private land throughout this area—respect the *No Trespassing* signs! Carry your Forest Service map—all the white area is private land. Often the public is allowed to pass through private land, but not to camp.

Nearest Services: Bring most of what you need with you, or stop in Pollock Pines for major groceries and bike parts. Gas, groceries, restaurant and bar are located at Ice House Resort. There is also a small motel and campground. The resort is located 9 miles in on Ice House Road. Ice House Resort is open in the winter, too, in case you want to cross-country ski in the area. Robb's Valley Resort is located 21 miles out Ice House Road with groceries, restaurant and bar.

ICE HOUSE AREA *Map 12*
10.3 miles on Ice House Road (1.3 miles past the resort), turn right at the Ice House Campground sign. Find a place to camp and relax. This

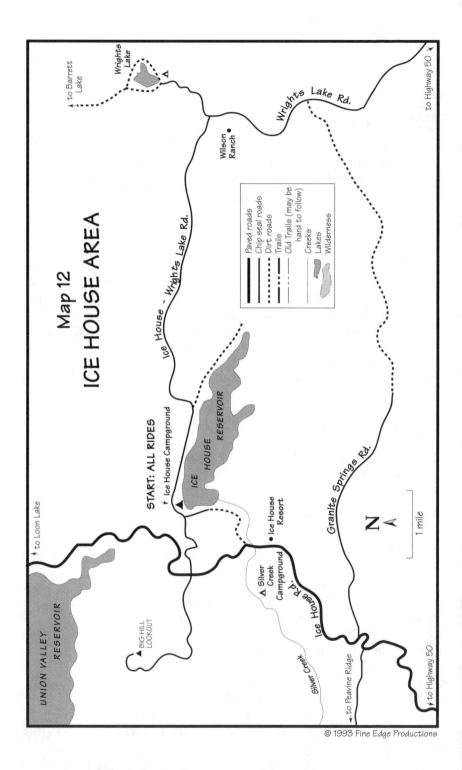

Map 12
ICE HOUSE AREA

© 1993 Fine Edge Productions

is a nice area for those who like "tame" conditions. Or for those of you travelling with friends with road bikes, there are several paved roads around.

Ride 1   Ice House Lakeshore
A scenic ride is to continue out the road to Wrights Lake on the paved road. In 2.2 miles, the paved road goes left towards Wrights Lake. Continue straight ahead on the dirt road until it ends after another 1.5 miles.

Ride 2   Ice House to Wrights Lake Out and Back
Ride out the paved road following the signs to Wrights Lake; this is Forest Service Road 32. This is a good steady climb—it's one of those rides that when you've had enough, just turn around and head back for camp and a swim! Total mileage from Ice House Reservoir to Wrights Lake and back is approximately 22 miles.

Ride 3   Big Hill Lookout
This is another paved surface ride. Ride back out the road you drove in on, go across Ice House Road and ride up the Big Hill Lookout Road. Stay on the main road all the way to the top, go past the Forest Service Heliport (helicopter fire crew are stationed here) and ride on to the lookout tower. Climb the tower and have a look at all the terrain to be explored! Take your USFS map with you and spend some time orienting yourself. Then it's downhill back to the campground.

UNION VALLEY AREA   *Maps 13 & 14*
Continuing north on Ice House Road, 14 miles from Highway 50, you reach Union Valley Reservoir, the largest reservoir in the Crystal Basin Area. Several Forest Service campgrounds are located all along the shore of Union Valley Reservoir, with dirt roads surrounding them. For rides closest to Union Valley see Bassi and Two Peaks Ride, or Van Fleck Area/ Shadow Lake.

Robb's Peak Lookout
One unique camping opportunity is to stay at the Robb's Hut located at Robb's Peak Lookout. The Robb's Hut is an abandoned fire lookout that has been converted into a hut. Rather than tear down the lookout, a few dedicated Forest Service employees and volunteers from R.E.I in Sacramento converted the out building into a hut. The hut can be rented for $15.00 a night—be sure to book far in advance through the Forest

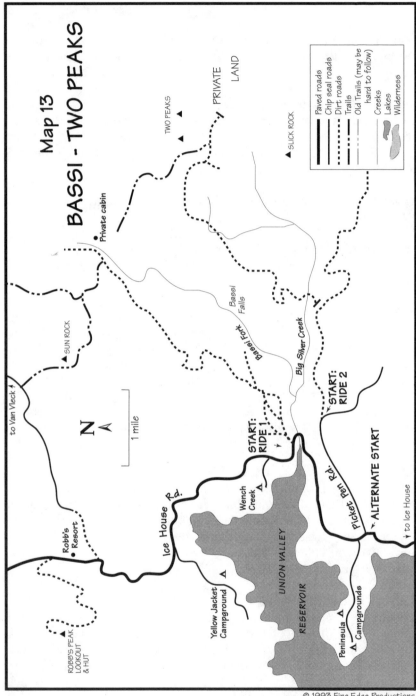

Map 13
BASSI - TWO PEAKS

TWO PEAKS

PRIVATE
LAND

SLICK ROCK

Paved roads
Chip seal roads
Dirt roads
Trails
Old Trails (may be
hard to follow)
Creeks
Lakes
Wilderness

Private cabin

SUN ROCK

to Van Vleck

N

1 mile

Bassi Fork

Bassi
Falls

Big Silver Creek

START:
RIDE 1

START:
RIDE 2

Robb's
Resort

Ice House Rd.

Wench
Creek

Picket Pen Rd.

ALTERNATE START

to Ice House

ROBB'S PEAK
LOOKOUT
& HUT

Yellow Jacket
Campground

UNION VALLEY

RESERVOIR

Peninsula
Campgrounds

© 1993 Fine Edge Productions

Service Information Center in Camino, telephone number 916-644-6048. Usable year-round, in winter it becomes a cross-country ski hut. A problem with mountain biking from the lookout is that all the riding begins with a downhill and ends with an uphill. Another problem with biking off Robb's Peak is that you don't get very far in any direction before you run into private land with closed, gated roads and No Trespassing signs. But if you are looking for a private place to hang-out, reserve the hut and you'll enjoy it. The hut is 21.3 miles from Highway 50, and 0.3 mile past Robb's Resort.

Southfork Campground

22.6 miles from Highway 50, on Ice House Road is the turnoff for Southfork Campground, located on the south fork of the Rubicon River. There is still exploring left to do out here. The older topo maps show lots of trails in this area, some have been reclaimed and reopened but there are others out there to discover. Be careful if you explore this area because the trails that lead down to the Rubicon River can be quite steep!

BASSI-TWO PEAKS AREA *Map 13*
Ride 1   Bassi Out and Back

Elevation: 5,000'–6,194' at Upper Bassi.
Mileage: Out and Back Ride—10 miles.
Level of Difficulty: Intermediate to advanced.
Water: Bassi fork of Silver Creek at the half way point runs year round but can be quite low in late August. Be sure to filter all your water.

The Drive: 16 miles north of Highway 50 on Ice House Road, turn right on the dirt road just after you cross Big Silver Creek. (2.3 miles past the turn off to Peninsula Campground). Park anywhere out of the way.
The Ride: Take any one of the first three roads to the left (real jeep roads, not straight up skid trails). Don't be tricked into taking any of the spur roads that climb to the left—they go up very steeply, then turn to skid trails, then end. Continue on the main road that runs northeast. 0.9 mile: Continue on into a meadow area. 1.3 miles: Now it is time to go left and start the climb. 2.0 miles: Go left again (right turn takes you to a view spot). 2.3 miles: After a cobbled section, a road enters on the left from Wench Flat, stay right. There are two more cobbled, stream bottom sections, then the road becomes much smoother and continues climbing. The entire climb is rideable, if you hit it with the right road conditions.

3.1 miles: You'll reach an opening on the ridge with a good look at Slick

Rock (the smooth granite rock) and Two Peaks to the southeast. When you are ready to continue, go left dropping onto the north side of the ridge. This next section, where the road re-enters the forest, can be one meadow bog after another. When in doubt, carry your bike around the bad spots. If you can't ride on the road, either turn around, go back and try again in a few weeks when things dry out, or *carry* your bike around the bad spots. Please don't leave any mountain bike tire tracks out in the meadow. Use good judgment; this is a sensitive area, part of which is private land. If it is too wet, turn back. There are plenty of other roads to explore.

5 miles: You reach Upper Bassi, which is private land, as you ride along the fence line. When you get to where the fence crosses the river crossing, stop and look directly behind you—you will see new trail blazes marking the Sun Rock Trail. This trail is rideable and takes you either to Sun Rock and Van Fleck Road or to the Van Fleck Ranch. *Caution:* Horseback riders use these trails so ride safely! For many of the horseback riders, this may be their first time on a mountain trail, and it may be their first encounter with a mountain bike. Make sure it is a good experience!

If you are looking for a good picnic spot, ride on the jeep road for about a half mile farther. The road begins to disappear, then ends at a nice camp spot. All along the creek you should be able to find suitable picnic sites. The table-top granite along the creek is fun to explore. After lunch, slab riding, wading and maybe some swimming, follow the road back downhill. Don't forget the cobbled sections! Remember, part of this ride travels through private land. Please stay on the road.

Ride 2   Two Peaks Hill Climb   *Map 13*

Topo Maps: 7.5 min. Loon Lake; small part of Kyburz.
Mileage: 12 miles from Ice House Road.
Water: Several small creeks, but carry all you need from Big Silver Creek on.
Level of Difficulty: Most cyclists who enjoy this ride are advanced, both in physical condition and technical skills.
Elevation: 5,000'–7,000'.

This is one of those rides that just takes determination! I remember the first time I was talked into doing this ride, having only ridden a mountain bike a couple of times. I admit I was quite angry by the time I got to the top saying, "I just want to know WHY am I pushing my bike up a hill I have no intention of riding down!" They convinced me it was just like skiing, and I'd have no problem negotiating the turns. They were right,

High Sierra creek crossing

I loved it! Although I did stop a couple of times to rest my hands from braking so hard! I accomplished this ride as a physically strong, but technically weak rider.

The Drive: Drive out Ice House Road 14.2 miles from Highway 50, turn right on the Picket Pen Road. You could start your ride from here, if you want extra mileage, but we usually drive a bit farther. 1.5 miles on Picket Pen Road, turn left staying on Picket Pen Road. The road to the right goes to the U.S. Forest Service Stockpile. We usually park somewhere within the next mile.

The Ride: Ride—or continue driving—out Picket Pen Road. There is one gate to go through. Be sure you leave the gate as you found it, either open or closed. 2.3 miles out, you go to the left on the dirt road. (The road to the right is chip-sealed for a short distance.) At 0.3 mile, you'll reach a green gate (may or may not be there!). Ride around the gate and continue on. This section of the road passes through private land. Stay on the road. 0.2 mile: Cross the bridge over Big Silver Creek, then the climbing begins. It's 3.2 miles of steady uphill, starting at 5,280' and climbing to 7,000' at the top. Depending on the road conditions, it's all

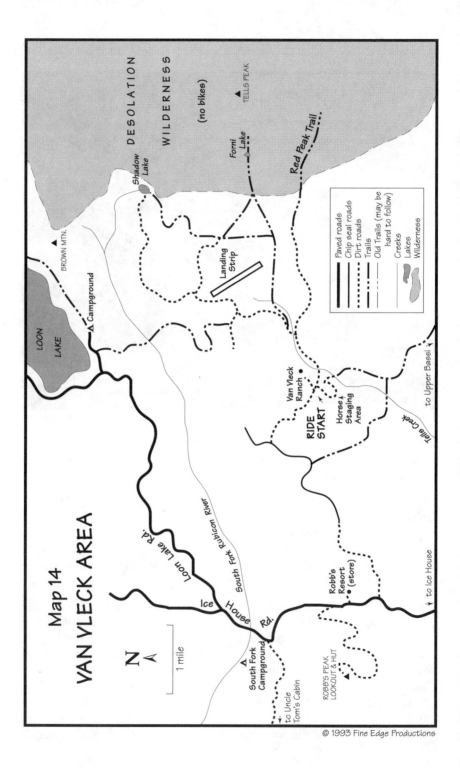

Map 14
VAN VLECK AREA

N

1 mile

DESOLATION
WILDERNESS
(no bikes)

TELLS PEAK ▲

Forni
Lake

Red Peak Trail

Shadow
Lake

BROWN MTN. ▲

△ Campground

LOON
LAKE

Landing
Strip

Loon Lake Rd.

South Fork Rubicon River

Van Vleck
Ranch ●

Horse ▲
Staging
Area

RIDE
START

Tells Creek

to Upper Basei

Legend:
Paved roads
Chip seal roads
Dirt roads
Trails
Old Trails (may be
hard to follow)
Creeks
Lakes
Wilderness

Ice House Rd.

South Fork
Campground △

to Uncle
Tom's Cabin

Robb's Resort
(store) ●

ROBB'S PEAK
LOOKOUT & HUT ▲

→ to Ice House

© 1993 Fine Edge Productions

rideable, although some may choose to walk some sections. 1.4 miles into the climb, where the road leaves the open and enters a forested area, look off to your right for three large-diameter Sugar Pine trees—the "Three Sisters." Walk over to the base and walk around them, to really appreciate their size!

You reach the top 1.8 miles after the trees! As you ride across the flat, look for a road to your right, which heads out to a vista point that's a good lunch and rest area. The road straight ahead is gated and is private land. At the vista point, get out your map and figure out where you are. The big lake to the west is Union Valley Reservoir and the rugged rocky peak behind you is Two Peaks. Check your brakes and tire pressure, lower your seat, then get ready for a fast downhill! Be careful of the waterbars in the lower half of the ride. Stop at the creek for a swim or rest, then ride back to your car. *Warning:* Please be careful. One mountain bike rider missed the bridge and flew off into Big Silver Creek. She is OK, but she had to be transported out by ambulance.

VAN VLECK AREA *Map 14*

The Drive: Drive out Ice House Road 20.6 miles to Robbs Saddle. Turn right at the sign *Crystal Basin Pack Station/Red Peak Trailhead.* Drive out this road that starts as dirt, then changes to pavement. 3.8 miles, the paved road goes straight ahead, but you go right. Follow the sign to the Pack Station. You could start your ride from any point, but we usually drive to the top. The road climbs from here. 1.5 miles: A corral is on the right. This is a good place to park, where you are out of the way. The other option is to drive on a bit farther and take the next right. Follow the sign to the horse staging area. Just before the staging area is the Wilderness Trail Parking Area with plenty of room for a group to park. The Van Vleck Area is unique in that it is gated Forest Service land with restricted use. The current policy is hikers (Desolation Trailhead), horseback riders and mountain bikes only—no motorized vehicles! Most of the area has a road system with room for multiple use without problems.

Caution: If you try any of the trails within this area, maintain a safe speed and dismount near all horseback riders and make sure hikers see you. Socialize, and show everyone that the multiple use policy will work. This is a bit of an experiment, because the area is not heavily used by any recreational group, so be a responsible rider. Think about those of us who live here, and want to continue riding this area!

Most of the roads here provide out-and-back rides for mountain bikes, because Desolation Wilderness is located to the east. The classic mountain bike ride for this area is the "Shadow Lake Ride," which I consider a challenging beginner ride. Beginners may walk a couple of uphill pitches, but just when you start to get tired, you arrive at the lake. After a swim and a snack, spirits are usually high for the downhill journey to the car!

Shadow Lake

Topo Maps: 7.5 min. Loon Lake. Start: T13N, R15E, section 32.
Mileage: 10 miles total from the locked gate.
Level of Difficulty: Strong beginner or better.
Water: Tells Creek at the start, and at Shadow Lake. Filter or treat all water.
Elevation: 6,500'–7,240'.

The Ride: Continue out the road you drove in on to get to the green gate. Go around the gate and continue on. Off to the left across the meadow is the Van Vleck Ranch, pack station and occasional winter ski hut! 0.7 mile: At a "Y" intersection, stay to the left. The road to the right goes to the Red Peak Trailhead. As you start to climb, be on the lookout for a green walk-through gate and several take-down fences across the road. Be sure to leave the gates as you found them! Continue on the main road, past a couple of roads that enter on the left. The road then turns eastward a bit and continues climbing. 1.7 miles: You'll see a large flat grassy/dirt area—this is the landing strip shown on the topo map. Continue straight ahead, as the road turns to the north again. This next section can be a bit tough, depending on how much horse traffic has been through here. Short, steep ups and downs are no problem if the traction is good, but sometimes the horses travel in the best line, and traction is terrible! 0.8 mile, turn right (uphill) at the next intersection. (To the left is a rocky ride down to the south fork of the Rubicon River.) If you look to the north while you climb the next section, the lake you see is Loon Lake.

The road levels out and is grassy in spots. Continue on the road which deteriorates to a trail. Shadow Lake is to the east, and uphill from you. You should end up on the edge of a drainage. If you look across it, you should see trail markers (red dots and ducks—a duck is a pile of at least 3 rocks, one on top of the other). If you're not into trail riding or portaging your bike, grab your lunch and water bottle, stash your bikes and hike the last quarter mile to the lake. Take a swim and have lunch. Then enjoy the mostly downhill ride back to your car. Don't forget the gates, if they were up!

LOON LAKE AREA *Map 15*

The Loon Lake turnoff is located 23.7 miles from the highway, or 1.1 mile past Southfork Campground. The Loon Lake Campground is located 4.3 miles from the turnoff. The elevation is 6,378'. This is a favorite camping spot in the Crystal Basin area. A lot of exploring can be done from this campground.

Ride 1   Loon Lake Trail

Mileage: Out and back 7 miles
Level of Difficulty: Beginning trail riding.

Look for the Wilderness Trailhead located in the campground—the Desolation Wilderness boundary is about 6.5 miles away. This trail is only about 3.5 miles long, but is one of the "funnest" around. It follows along the lake, so for once you get to ride on a trial that isn't all up, then all down! I recommend this one for people just getting started in trail riding. Although there are short, steep ups, most of the trail is gentle so you can concentrate on obstacle negotiation, learning how to pick up the front of the bike and how to move the bike around. Just remember you are on a trailhead to Desolation Wilderness, so you will encounter hikers and horseback riders. If you do, *it is best to get off your bike and stand out of the way of the horses.*

After about 3.5 miles, the trail ends turning into a gravel road. Your options from here are to turn around and ride back, continue one-half mile to Pleasant Campground, or continue following the directions of the loop ride.

Ride 2   The Slabs

Mileage: Out and back 8 miles.
Level of Difficulty: Intermediate or better.

From Loon Lake Campground, ride out to the main road a half mile, turn right on the Loon Lake Road and continue across the first dam and on to the second spillway dam. 2.8 miles: Cross the dam and go left on the jeep road that goes down toward Gerle Creek. Look to your right and stay on the jeep road as it climbs a bit and goes around the ridge.

The next section can be quite confusing as the jeepers have created several roads, all ending up in the same place. Next, you see a large mud puddle, occasionally with a jeep stuck in it. It is easy for mountain bikers to negotiate this section which at times can be irritating to the jeepers! Just a little bit farther, and you are out on the granite slabs! Slab riding

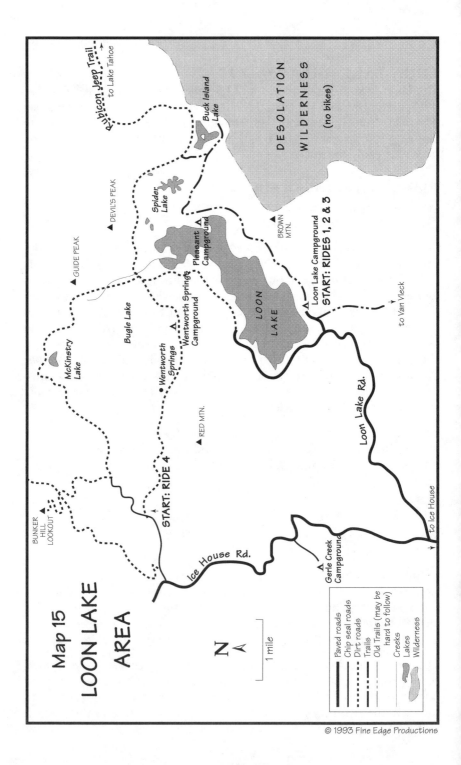

Map 15
LOON LAKE
AREA

N

1 mile

Paved roads
Chip seal roads
Dirt roads
Trails
Old Trails (may be hard to follow)
Creeks
Lakes
Wilderness

DESOLATION WILDERNESS (no bikes)

Rubicon Jeep Trail
to Lake Tahoe

Buck Island Lake

▲ DEVIL'S PEAK

Spider Lake

▲ GUIDE PEAK

▲ BROWN MTN.

Pleasant Campground

LOON LAKE

Loon Lake Campground
START: RIDES 1, 2 & 3

to Van Vleck

McKinstry Lake

Bugle Lake

Wentworth Springs Campground

● Wentworth Springs

Loon Lake Rd.

▲ RED MTN.

START: RIDE 4

BUNKER HILL LOOKOUT ▲

Ice House Rd.

Gerle Creek Campground

to Ice House

© 1993 Fine Edge Productions

is another technique that improves your bike handling skills. It can also be death to rims, pedals and chain rings! *Be careful!* Slab riding is a bit like back-country telemark skiing, make a few turns, hop around an obstacle or two, then another quick turn into the hill in hopes of regaining some of the elevation you just lost! When you've had enough, ride back to the campground.

Ride 3   Loon Lake Loop

Topo maps: 7.5 min Loon Lake, Wentworth Springs.
Mileage: 16 miles.
Elevation: 6,400'–6,780'.
Level of Difficulty: This ride is suggested only for those in good physical condition, with the right state of mind and solid technical skills. You need to be the kind of rider who doesn't mind pushing his/her bike in order to enjoy the beauty of this area. This ride will also give you an idea of what the terrain in Desolation Wilderness is like. I consider this ride a classic, but it's not for everyone. If you have doubts, try the McKinstry Lake Loop. If you enjoy the first 5 miles of that ride, give this one a try!

From the Loon Lake Campground, look for the wilderness trailhead and ride out the trail to the upper end of the lake (for details see Ride 1). At 3.5 miles, the trail crosses a creek and goes uphill. The trail ends and a gravel road begins. Sounds simple, but this is no ordinary gravel road. Most of the roadbed has rather large rocks. At 0.5 mile, the trail takes off to the left to Pleasant Campground. Not heavily used, this could be a good bike-in campground. The road surface begins to improve when the climbing is through! Follow the road as it leaves the lake.

2.8 miles: After a short rideable section, the road turns back to rocks and cobbles for a technical downhill. You may prefer to walk some of this section. When the trail reenters the trees, look for a signpost without a sign (some day there might be a new sign). Remember this spot, as you will want to return here after you ride the last 0.1 mile down to the lake. You are now 6 miles from the start of the ride, so enjoy the lake and take the time to pull out your maps to see where you are and where you are supposed to go next.

To complete the loop, go back to the signpost and follow the trail (0.6 mile to jeep road) that contours a bit then drops down to the creek. You can see the jeep road from here, just make your way over to it. After a short rideable stretch, the road becomes pretty amazing! You are now on the Rubicon Jeep Trail, a high country jeep trail that goes all the way across the Sierra, ending at the shore of Lake Tahoe. Several times through the next uphill section, you will question yourself as to who talked you into this ride (push).

The trail continues to climb, sometimes rideable, sometimes it's just easier to push. After one last uphill, you see roads and trails heading off to the left that lead to Spider Lake. Continue on the main road for 1.5 miles to Little Sluice Box. This section of trail is completely composed of large rocks. Funny, jeeps can negotiate spots like this! Fortunately, with a bike you can portage around this spot. The road becomes more rideable now, with the bad sections always becoming shorter and shorter.

Eventually you cross Ellis Creek. Just a little farther (0.1 mile), take the jeep trail that goes left toward Loon Lake. The Rubicon Jeep Trail continues straight ahead here heading to Wentworth Springs. Your spirits will rise through this next section. For most people their second wind (or third or fourth) kicks in about now, as the terrain becomes more rideable. 0.7 mile later you reach a muddy section. One trail leads to one of the biggest natural mud holes I've ever seen! Fortunately, on a bike you can easily get around this obstacle!

Continue on to the slabs, a large, open granite field. Don't get tricked into riding all the way down to the bottom. It's fun, but you need to stay fairly high and to the left up toward the trees, and you'll find the road again. 1.4 miles later go around the ridge and then you end up at the spillway. Ride up to the dam and cross it. Stay on the paved Loon Lake Road back to the campground, 3.2 miles away. You are on your own when you go on this ride! Go with the right frame of mind and you'll love it—it's all up to you! But be warned, it's not easy!

Ride 4   McKinstry Lake Loop
Topo Maps: 7.5 min. Wentworth Springs. Start: T14N, R14E, section 35.
Mileage: 12+ miles total.
Water: Ellis Creek, 5 mile point. Treat all water before drinking.
Level of Difficulty: Intermediate or better, but don't be fooled by the low mileage! There are small, technical trials sections for those seeking challenge.
Elevation: 5,700'–7,040'.

The Drive: Drive out Ice House Road 28.4 miles from Highway 50 (4.7 miles past the Loon Lake Road). Turn right on the road to Wentworth Springs and Bunker Hill Lookout. Continue straight ahead, 1.6 miles, to where the paved road goes left and the Wentworth Springs Road goes straight ahead and turns to gravel. Park here, where the road crosses Bart's Creek.

The Ride: Ride out the dirt, sand, gravel and rock road that goes straight ahead. This road, also known as the Rubicon Jeep Trail, goes all the way across the Sierra ending at Lake Tahoe in Tahoma. 2 miles out you pass through private land. Stay on your bike and ride 1.5 miles to Wentworth Springs Campground. The road is rough in spots and it gives you a taste of the Rubicon Jeep Trail. A half mile past the campground, you come to a spot where the roads go in all directions. Just remember: all roads to the south (hard rights) lead to Loon Lake. Take any of the roads that go straight ahead, or to the left (uphill). The uphill part is a definite challenge, with most people walking short sections, but it is still more rideable than not. Next, the jeep trail takes you out on a granite slab. If you've never ridden on granite, you will be amazed at the traction your tires get. If you have problems following the road across the slabs, look down on the granite for the oil spots the jeeps leave behind.

When the road enters the forest and levels out, look for a road taking off to the left. The easiest way to be sure this is the right road is to continue on the Rubicon Jeep Trail to Ellis Creek, a good rest spot and place to refill your water bottles. *Be sure to filter or treat all water.*

Take the road you saw just before reaching Ellis Creek, and continue uphill toward Guide Peak. After 1 mile you arrive at an intersection, with a road going straight up the draw. Turn right here, go across the drainage, then up along the base of Guide Peak. Both roads get there, but the road to the right is not as steep and is easier to ride. 1.2 miles later: This leads you up to a saddle with McKinstry Peak and the Red Cliffs straight ahead, This road curves west then drops down to McKinstry Lake, a nice rest stop. This is private land, so as nice as it looks—*No Camping Allowed!* Continue on the road you came in on, for the final 100 foot elevation gain of the ride. Then the downhill begins! 3.2 miles: When you reach the paved road, turn left for a faster downhill back to your car 2 miles away.

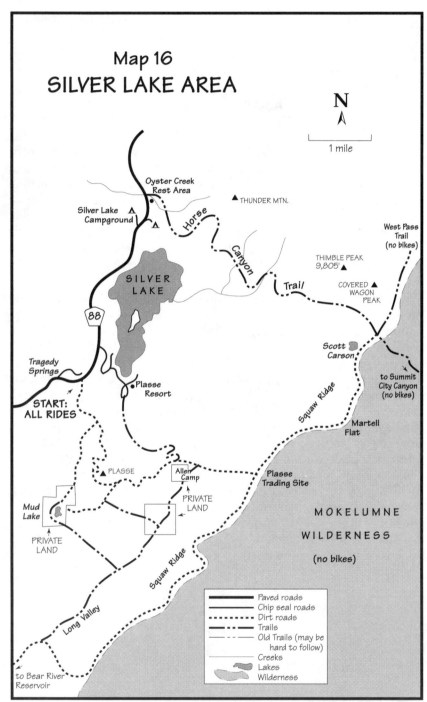

Map 16
SILVER LAKE AREA

N

1 mile

Oyster Creek
Rest Area

▲ THUNDER MTN.

Silver Lake
Campground

Horse

Canyon

West Pass
Trail
(no bikes)

THIMBLE PEAK
9,805' ▲

Trail

COVERED ▲
WAGON
PEAK

SILVER
LAKE

88

Scott
Carson

to Summit
City Canyon
(no bikes)

Tragedy
Springs

Plasse
Resort

START:
ALL RIDES

Squaw Ridge

Martell
Flat

▲ PLASSE

Allen
Camp

Plasse
Trading Site

PRIVATE
LAND

Mud
Lake

MOKELUMNE

PRIVATE
LAND

Squaw Ridge

WILDERNESS

(no bikes)

Long Valley

Paved roads
Chip seal roads
Dirt roads
Trails
Old Trails (may be
hard to follow)
Creeks
Lakes
Wilderness

to Bear River
Reservoir

© 1993 Fine Edge Productions

5 HIGHWAY 88 AREA

Tragedy Springs/Mud Lake Loop; Tragedy Springs to Silver Lake; Horse Canyon/Carson Mormon-Emigrant Trail

Highway 88 is a scenic highway that runs west to east across the Sierra at Carson Pass. Highway 88 is south of U.S. 50, and north of Highway 4. Most of the rides in this area are above 7,000', so you have to save these until the snow melts. Even in a dry year you may find patches of snow and wet conditions in June. This area is very sensitive, so be sure the roads and trails are open and dry enough that you don't damage the environment. The southern boundary of most of the riding in this area is in the Mokelumne Wilderness. *No bikes allowed!*

Seasons: July–October, unless there is an early autumn snowstorm.
Camping: Several U.S. Forest Service and PG&E campgrounds are located along Highway 88. My favorites are the ones by Silver Lake and Caples Lake. Small cabins can be rented at both Silver and Caples Lakes.
Nearest Services: Motels, condominiums and cabins can be rented at Kirkwood Ski area. Small stores, gas stations and restaurants are located all along Highway 88. Bring major supplies with you. Closest bike shops are in South Lake Tahoe.

SILVER LAKE AREA *Map 16*

Ride 1   Tragedy Springs/Mud Lake Loop

Topo Maps: 7.5 min. Tragedy Springs; Bear River Reservoir. Start: T9N, R17E, section 7.
Mileage: 7 miles. Short loop to get you used to the elevation.
Elevation: 7,900'–8,300'.
Level of Difficulty: Beginner

The Drive: Drive east on Highway 88, and 5 miles past Mormon Emigrant Trail (just before you reach Silver Lake), turn right on Mud Lake Road opposite Tragedy Springs. (If you get to Plasse's Resort Rd., you missed Mud Lake Road and must go back one mile.) Park out of the way of the summer homes, one-half mile up Mud Lake Road from Highway 88 near the sign reading *Mud Lake 2 miles.* This is also an entrance to Mokelumne Wilderness, so if there is no place to park go across the highway and park at Tragedy Springs, then ride back to this point.

Roadside R & R

The Ride: Ride out the jeep road 1.2 miles, turn right on the jeep road to Mud Lake. In places the jeeps have gone several different ways, usually avoiding mud holes, so just follow the road most travelled. 1.2 miles later the road splits, go right 0.3 mile to Mud Lake. Mud Lake is located on private land. You can ride through, but no camping. When you are done exploring the lake, ride back 0.3 mile to the last intersection to continue the loop ride. The road follows the creek for about a mile, then climbs back up on the ridge towards Plasse. 1.4 miles farther, there should be a sign that reads *Tragedy Springs [left]; Highway 88 [left]; Plasses [right]*. Go left towards Tragedy Springs and Highway 88. In 2.2 miles you are back at your car.

Ride 2   Tragedy Springs/Mud Lake Loop
(Trail Version)

Mileage: 9 miles. Not long but you'll walk sections and occasionally wonder
where you are.
Level of Difficulty: Strong beginners or better.

The Ride: A very scenic ride, but only for adventurers carrying a map and
compass! Follow Ride 1 to Mud Lake. Continue around the lake in a
counter clockwise direction. The trail you are looking for takes off from
the spillway at the south end of the lake. Following the trail around the
lake at times is frustrating, just keep heading toward the spillway and
you'll pick up the trail there.

After crossing the creek once, the trail goes around the ridge, then
follows Bear River. The trail is hard to follow through here. It has been
flagged for trail work but there is little money for trails these days, so it
may be hard to follow for quite some time. The best suggestion is to carry
7.5 min. topo maps! Depending on what time of year it is, you may cross
2 or 3 tributaries of Bear River, then the trail continues southeast about
0.3 mile to an intersection; turn left up Long Valley. The trail heads north
and after about 1.3 miles it turns into an abandoned jeep road that
intersects with a jeep road. (Left takes you back to Mud Lake.) Go right
towards Allen Camp. Here the jeep roads loop around Allen Camp and
it may get confusing at times. Follow the signs back to the northwest
towards Highway 88 at Tragedy Springs.

Ride 3   Tragedy Springs to Silver Lake

Mileage: 8+ miles.
Level of Difficulty: Technical downhill section for intermediate riders. It is fun, if
you know how to use your brakes and stay under control.

The Ride: Follow the Mud Lake 4-wheel drive road to Plasse. Continue
straight ahead towards Allen Camp. Just before the road drops off to
Allen Camp, look left on the ridge for the motorcycle trail signs. Follow
the trail to the top of the ridge and get ready for a great view of Silver
Lake. It is approximately 4.5 miles from Highway 88 to the motorcycle
trail. Most people will have to walk the first two switchbacks, but from
then on this trail is rideable for mountain bikes. *Be alert!* This trail is used
by motorcycles, horseback riders and hikers. It is easy to pick up too
much speed in several sections. Be a safe rider, maintain a controllable
speed and don't skid your turns!

After 2.5 miles of downhill and dropping 1,000 feet, you end up at yet another settlement known as Plasse. This time it is a resort, campground area. Slow down and ride cautiously. The road turns to pavement and you are now travelling through private land. Continue up the pavement to Highway 88. Turn left and pump uphill 0.8 mile back to your car. One option is to send the drivers uphill to get the vehicles and everyone else turn right and peddle downhill to Silver Lake Resort for refreshments.

Singletracking through a pleasant meadow

Ride 4   Horse Canyon/ Carson-Mormon Emigrant Trail

Topo Maps: 7.5 min. Caples Lake; Tragedy Springs; Mokelumne Peak; Bear River Reservoir. Start: Tragedy Springs T9N, R17E, section 7.
Mileage: 14.5 miles dirt & trail; 18.5 if you complete the loop on pavement.
Water: None in the first 9 miles. When you reach the Horse Canyon Trail, the creek at the top runs through July but can be dry by the end of summer. Treat all water.
Level of Difficulty: Expert riders only. If you doubt your climbing ability, try Rides 1 or 2 to see how you deal with the elevation and climbing.
Elevation: 7,200'–9,000'.
Season: Mid-June through mid-October.

This is one of the all-time great trails and jeep road rides. The entire ride is from 7,200' to just over 9,000'. Cyclists can enjoy a high alpine experience while following one of the original pioneer trails. This trail, called the Carson-Mormon Emigrant Trail, has been marked with monuments made from railroad irons. If you see them, they're worth stopping to read. This ride is only for those of you who enjoy beautiful high alpine terrain, incredible wildflowers and don't mind walking and pushing your bike a bit to get there. You climb from 7,200' to over 9,000' in 9 miles. Much of this is rideable, except for a few short steep uphill sections. The best way to do this ride is to leave one vehicle at Oyster Creek Picnic Area, at the Silver Lake Campgrounds, or somewhere by Silver Lake on Highway 88. This eliminates 4 miles of mostly uphill on pavement. Drive or ride your bikes to Tragedy Springs opposite Mud Lake Road and just southwest of Silver Lake on Highway 88.

The Ride: From Highway 88, turn south on Mud Lake Road, across the Highway from Tragedy Springs. 2.6 miles: Go left at the sign that says *Allen Camp 2 miles.* (The road to the right goes to Mud Lake.) 1.2 miles later: Look off to your left and you'll see a motorcycle trail that goes down to Silver Lake. (See Tragedy Springs to Silver Lake Ride.) 0.3 mile farther you reach Allen Camp. All that is left is an old cabin at the edge of the meadow. This is private land, so please stay on the designated roads through the area. Continue on the newer road (the one not blocked off) which keeps you out of most of the mud. After 1.3 miles of climbing you reach Squaw Ridge. (A right down Squaw Ridge leads to Bear River Reservoir, also a good ride if you leave a car at the reservoir for a shuttle.) Along the ridge you should see monuments (made of railroad iron) giving historical information about the Mormon-Carson Emigrant Trail of 1848. The road you are riding on is an actual wagon route used to settle the lands farther to the west. As you climb higher in elevation and start huffing and puffing for oxygen, think about how it was to get a wagon over some of the rocky stretches! All the way up the ridge you are on the edge of the Mokelumne Wilderness Area. All roads and trails to the south (right) are closed to mechanized vehicles! *Please keep your bike on the road.*

3.5 miles later you're at the top and the end of the road that's open to mountain bikes. Hike over to the Wilderness Boundary and take a look down Summit City Canyon. Take a break, then follow the motorcycle signs for the Horse Canyon Trail. (Turn left at the vehicle closure sign.) The first three-quarters of a mile is rough following the creek bed, but after that the trail is a blast with only occasional rough spots! Take a topo map along so you can pick out Thimble Peak and Covered Wagon Peak. This is the back side of Kirkwood Ski Resort. 5 miles later you'll reach Highway 88. Turn left on 88 towards Silver Lake and ride back to where you parked your car. This ride can also be done in reverse, starting from Oyster Creek Picnic Area, riding up the Horse Canyon Trail and down the jeep road. The motorcycle trail is more rideable in the downhill direction, but this loop is fun and spectacular in either direction!

Pine cone stop

6 HOPE VALLEY AREA

Indian Valley; Upper Blue Lake to Lost Lakes; Deer Valley;
Red Lake to Lost Lakes; Red Lake/Blue Lake Loop;
Burnside Lake

This is a good spot to come with a family or a group of riders with differing ability levels. Easy out and back rides are no problem to design. Tougher rides can be found by heading north to Lost Lakes or south to Deer Valley and Highway 4. Swimming, fishing and hiking is available for mixed recreation. It can be crowded here on weekends, but mid-week is pretty quiet. For convenience, the first three rides start from Lower Blue Lakes Campground.

The Drive: Blue Lakes Road is located in Hope Valley 6.5 miles east of Carson Pass or 3 miles west of Picketts Junction (intersection Highway 89 from South Lake Tahoe) on Highway 88. Turn south on Blue Lakes Road. The road is paved about 6 miles then turns to dirt and gravel. For extra mileage all of these rides can begin from where the gravel and dirt begins, or back at Highway 88.

Camping: Three campgrounds, operated by PG&E, are located near the lakes in the area.

Nearest Services: East on Highway 88, 3.5 miles to Sorensen's Resort, with a small store, cabins, etc. For major supplies, go north on Highway 89 at Pickett's Junction to South Lake Tahoe. Closest bike shops: South Lake Tahoe.

Seasons: June through October, or until the first snow.

BLUE LAKES AREA *Map 17*
Ride 1 Indian Valley

Topo Maps: 7.5 min. Carson Pass; Pacific Valley. 15 min. Markleeville. Start: T9N, R19E, section 30.
Mileage: 11 miles round trip.
Level of Difficulty: Easy, beginning mountain bike riding, all on dirt roads.

From Lower Blue Lakes Campground, ride to the Blue Lakes Road, turn left and continue to the road to Tamarack Lake, Summit Lake, Upper Sunset, Wet Meadows, etc. Turn right and ride out the dirt road, passing Tamarack Lake on your left first. Either detour to the lake or continue straight ahead. Next you pass the road to Upper and Lower Sunset Lakes, once again either detour to the lakes, or continue on to Indian Valley. The road continues about 1.5 miles further, then you run into the Wilderness Boundary and have to stop. Even though this is a short out and back ride, the scenery is well worth it! Indian Valley is a small valley with a meandering creek—this is a great place to enjoy the fall colors. Everything turns golden against the rocks and blue sky.

Ride 2   Upper Blue Lake to Lost Lakes

Mileage: 4 miles to Lost Lake. The loop out to Highway 88 via Blue Lakes Road is approximately 23 miles.
Level of Difficulty: For strong beginners, a non-technical scenic run.

The Ride: Continue out Upper Blue Lakes Road to Upper Blue Lake, about 1.5 miles. Continue riding around the lake following the signs to the campground. To go to Lost Lakes, continue on the main road that goes past the turn off to Upper Blue Lakes Campground. 0.8 mile, turn right and ride out to Lost Lakes, enjoy the views! Either ride back to your camp, or switch to the Red Lake/

Ranch house, Blue Lakes Road

Lost Lake Ride for a longer ride. With pavement riding, it is possible to make a loop out of this one. Blue Lakes, Lost Lakes, Red Lake; right on Highway 88, another right on Blue Lakes Road back to your camp.

Ride 3   Deer Valley

Mileage: Hermit Valley and back—approximately 9 miles each way.
Elevation: 8,055'–7,100'.
Level of Difficulty: Intermediate to advanced if you go all the way to Hermit Valley. It is for strong beginners if you skip the last part of the ride.

This is a classic jeep road that so far has been allowed to remain as a corridor through the Mokelumne Wilderness Area. Stay on the road and out of the Wilderness Area. This ride is a good one to try out your mountain bike camping skills. The ride to Hermit Valley and Highway 4 is only 9 miles, but it is one of those spots where you feel like you are a long way out.

The Ride: From the campground at Lower Blue Lake ride back to the main road. Turn right toward Twin and Meadow Lakes. 0.1 mile turn south (left) on the jeep road to Deer Valley and Hermit Valley. First you descend into Clover Valley following Blue Creek. You cross Blue Creek in the middle of Clover Valley, then continue on. After leaving Clover Valley, you descend into Deer Valley, with Deer Creek running through it. The road forks along Deer Creek. Stay to the left to continue on to Hermit Valley. (The right fork is now within the Mokelumne Wilderness.) If you look carefully in Deer Valley, you may see the remains of an old sawmill.

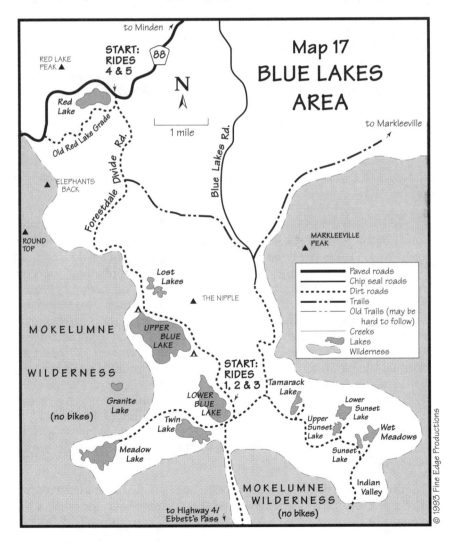

The trail climbs as it leaves Deer Valley. Once on the top, you need to decide what your plans are. Either turn around and ride back to Blue Lakes or descend 600+ feet down into Hermit Valley. This is a technical downhill and uphill section with lots of rocks. Ride as far as you want to, then turn around and follow your tracks back to Lower Blue Lake. This is another ride where it would be fun to get dropped off at the Blue Lakes (or Highway 88) and picked up on Highway 4 in Hermit Valley!

Ride 4   Red Lake to Lost Lakes

Maps: Start: T10, R18E, section 23.
Total Mileage: About 10 miles out and back.
Level of Difficulty: Intermediate riders.
Elevation: 7,800'–8,820'.
Camping: U.S. Forest Service campgrounds at Silver Lake and Caples Lake. PG&E campgrounds at Silver Lake or Blue Lakes. Cabins at Sorensen's Resort.
Nearest Services: Gas station and small store located at Sorensen's Resort, Kirkwood, or Caples Lake Resort.

The Drive: 2.5 miles east of Carson Pass on Highway 88, turn right at the road to Red Lake (the lake you see as you drive down the east side of the pass).

The Ride: After turning onto the road to Red Lake, immediately turn south (left) on the dirt road (Forestdale Divide Road ,which is #013.). The first 1.5 miles are relatively easy, a good warm-up for the climb. In July, the meadow to the left can be a dream for photographers or wildflower lovers. After you cross Forestdale Creek, the climbing begins. Nothing too technical, just a good, steep climb, gaining 840 feet in 1.5 miles to the top of Forestdale Divide. The view from this barren spot is unforgettable! Elephants Back and Round Top to the northwest, Markleeville Peak to the east. The view is so open and the sky so big all around, the mountain biker becomes small and insignificant! At the top you can see the signs for Mokelumne Wilderness and the Pacific Crest Trail. *Stay on the road and off the trail!* After shooting some pictures and enjoying the view, continue on the jeep road heading to Blue Lakes. 0.5 mile later you drop into the timber again. Be sure to look off to the right (west) for a spectacular view of Summit City Canyon and the Mokelumne Wilderness.

1.1 miles later, turn left on the road to Lost Lakes. There are two lakes up here. Ride out to the second one, then walk over to the edge of the canyon to the east. The rocks drop from 8,772' instantly to 8,000' to

Faith Valley. The large rock just to the south is the Nipple at 9,342'. Camping is allowed at Lost Lakes. Your option from here is to drop down the hill to Upper Blue Lake Campground a little less than a mile, or ride back the way you came. Be careful in the descent to Red Lake, the turns are sharper and the road surface is looser than you remember!

Ride 5   Red Lake/Blue Lake Loop

Total Mileage: 18 miles.
Level of Difficulty: Strong intermediate to advanced riders with good climbing skills and some singletrack experience.

The Ride: Start from Red Lake and follow the directions to Lost Lakes in Ride 4. Continue past Lost Lakes for a quick, steep mile to Upper Blue Lake and then continue past Lower Blue Lake. Turn left (east on Blue Lakes Road, which turns north and heads towards Highway 88. After a short climb the road descends into Charity Valley. Look to your right (east) for a trail going to Markleeville. Pass this trail and immediately and carefully look for a sign on the left (west) for a dirt road. It is hard to find, but worth it! Turn left onto this dirt road, which becomes singletrack trail. You ride on the trail and old jeep road for 3 miles, ending up back on Forestdale Divide Road. Turn right and ride back to your car. If you still feel like more mileage, try the old road around the south side of Red Lake. It's a steady climb for 1.75 miles, making for a fun downhill on the return. Great for fall color!

Burnside Lake   *Map 18*

Total Mileage: 13.6 miles round trip.
Level of Difficulty: Good trip to build endurance for intermediate or better riders.
Elevation: 7,056'–8,200'.
Topo Maps: 7.5 min. Carson Pass and Freel Peak.
Water: Basically none; cattle graze right by the lake.
Camping: Closest campgrounds are about 1 mile east on Highway 88.
Nearest Services: 14 miles northwest on Highway 89 to Meyers for major items. Small store, cabins for rent and restaurant a half miles east on 88 at Sorensen's Resort.

Highlight: You are very close to Grover Hot Springs and State Park (with campground) just out of the town of Markleeville. The hot springs can be a real treat after a day of riding. Go east on Highway 88, 5 miles, turn right on Highway 89 following the signs to Markleeville. Once in town, look for the Grover State Park sign—turn right and continue out to the park.

The Drive: This dirt road begins at Pickett's Junction on Highway 88,

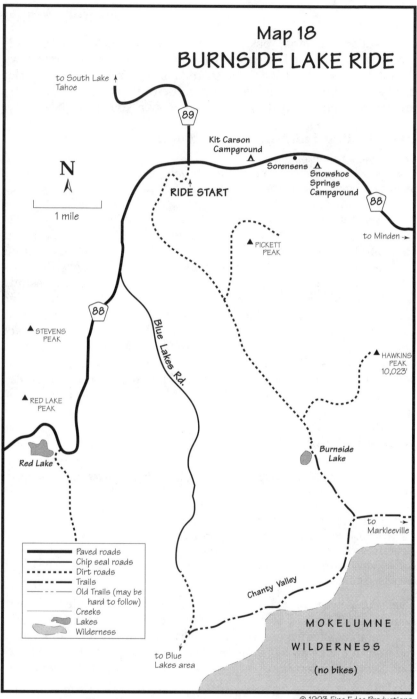

Map 18
BURNSIDE LAKE RIDE

to South Lake
Tahoe

89

Kit Carson
Campground

Sorensens

Snowshoe
Springs
Campground

88

RIDE START

to Minden →

N

1 mile

▲ PICKETT
PEAK

88

Blue Lakes Rd.

▲ STEVENS
PEAK

▲ HAWKINS
PEAK
10,023'

▲ RED LAKE
PEAK

Burnside
Lake

Red Lake

to
Markleeville

Chanty Valley

Paved roads
Chip seal roads
Dirt roads
Trails
Old Trails (may be
  hard to follow)
Creeks
Lakes
Wilderness

M O K E L U M N E

W I L D E R N E S S

to Blue
Lakes area

(no bikes)

© 1993 Fine Edge Productions

located at the base of Pickett Peak. This is the intersection of Highway 89 (14 miles to Meyers, Highway 50) and Highway 88. Take the dirt road south (just opposite from Highway 89). Park out of the way of through traffic. This area seems to be a popular dispersed camping spot during fishing and hunting season. It may look crowded, but hardly anyone goes out this road, except during deer season in the fall.

The Ride: The directions are easy! Follow the dirt road 6.2 miles to Burnside Lake. You can see roads taking off to the left that you may want to explore for extra mileage. Most of them climb quickly. At 3.2 miles: The road to the left contours around Pickett Peak. 5.7 miles: The road to the left is for the "Peak

Youngsters enjoy Sierra riding too!

Bagger" in the crowd. This road goes to Hawkins Peak, elevation 10,023' (1,800' of climbing). Don't attempt this on a hot day—there are no trees on Hawkins Peak! At 6.2 miles you reach Burnside Lake! If you continue on, the road turns into a trail. Good introductory trail riding for about 0.6 mile, where you end up on the canyon's edge. Markleeville is down below you. The view is worth it, even for those who would rather walk the 0.6 mile of trail. When you are done sight-seeing, ride back the way you came in.

From the overlook spot, Grover Hot Springs is at the end of this trail 2,000' below. It is only about a 3-mile descent, but most riders have to walk down some of the switchbacks. *Control your speed and watch out for hikers.* It may be enjoyable for some to ride the pavement from Grover Hot Springs (Highway 89, left on Highway 88) back to Pickett Junction, out to Burnside Lake, then down the trail back to the Hot Springs. I don't recommend this ride for most riders—only a few of the crazy downhillers, but there is a lot of uphill and pavement riding for only 3 miles of downhill!

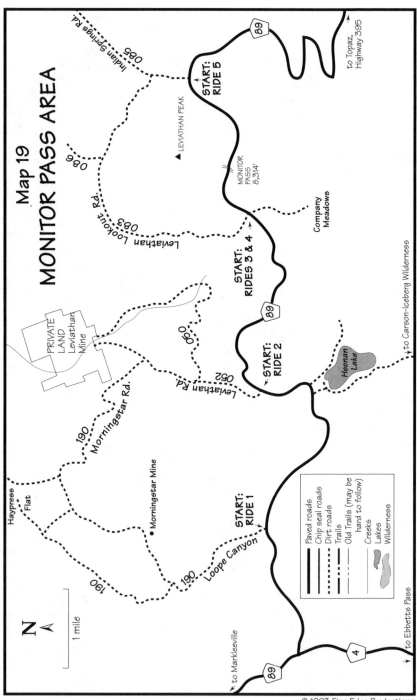

Map 19
MONITOR PASS AREA

© 1993 Fine Edge Productions

CHAPTER 7

MONITOR PASS AREA

Loope Canyon/Morningstar Loop; Leviathan Mine Loop;
Leviathan Peak Loop; Company Meadows; Indian Springs Road

MONITOR PASS AREA *Map 19*

In Eastern Alpine County, north of Highway 89 and the Nevada State line in the vicinity of Monitor Pass (8,314'), you can find some good, seldom-visited mountain biking routes. This area is a high lateral ridge of the Sierra and contains the southern flank of the East Fork of the Carson River as it meanders northeast into Nevada. Monitor Pass can be reached from Highway 395 on the east, or from State Highway 4 and Markleeville on the west.

During the fall months, late September to early November, the alpine trees on the 8,000' plateaus either side of Monitor Pass are a sight to see. At this elevation, the temperature is moderate on all but the hottest days of summer. However, water is scarce and shade comes only in batches on the margins of the meadows.

Camping: Grover Hot Springs State Park is located 5 miles west of the town of Markleeville. This is a great place to plan a mountain bike vacation! The park offers not only a campground but a hot springs pool to soak in after a long day of riding. Using Grover Hot Springs as a basecamp, you can easily ride one day in the Blue Lakes or Hope Valley Areas, then spend the next day exploring Monitor Pass. Camping is also available at the USFS Markleeville Campground, located 0.7 mile south of Markleeville on the banks of Markleeville Creek.

Services and Facilities: Gas, grocery stores and restaurants can all be found in Markleeville, but bring the bulk of your supplies with you, including bike tools and spare tubes. The closest bike shops are in South Lake Tahoe to the northwest or in Gardnerville and Minden to the northeast. Both areas are over 30 miles away.

The Drive: Starting in the center of Markleeville, head south on State Routes 4 and 89, following the Carson River East Fork upstream. At 0.7 mile you can see the turnoff for Markleeville Campground on the left. 2.3 miles: East Fork Resort with cabins on the river. 4.8 miles: Junction of State Route 4 and 89. Turn left (east) on Highway 89. 6.3 miles: Pass through a mining excavation area. 6.6 miles: Continue up the paved road. The dirt road to the left (sharp turn, sign says *Loope Canyon*) is USFS

Route 190, Loope Canyon to Haypress Flat. 8.8 miles: Dirt road to the right goes to Heenan Lake Wildlife Area. 9.6 miles: Dirt road to the left is USFS Route 052, the end of the Haypress Flat Loop and Leviathan Mine Loop (see below). The road to the right (south) heads to Company Meadows and BLM land on the county line. 10.1 miles: Stone marker on the right marks the summit of Monitor Pass 8,314'. This is the last of the five Sierra passes which are part of the famous Markleeville Death Ride, a bike ride sponsored by the Markleeville Chamber of Commerce.

Ride 1   Loope Canyon/Morningstar Loop

This is a moderately strenuous loop through a variety of terrain. From 1.8 miles east of State Route 4 on Highway 89, reset your odometer to 0.0 and head steeply uphill on USFS Route 190, following Loope Canyon (see above). This is a well-graded road which serves a number of mines in the area. 0.7 mile: The road to the left is a mining road. 1.2 miles: You reach the head of Loope Canyon. Stay on the main road which climbs the ridge to the northeast. 1.7 miles: You cross a saddle and drop down into Morningstar Canyon. At the bottom of the canyon a road turns left to Haypress Flat. Stay right, heading up the canyon, climbing steeply to the east. As you pass the Morningstar Mine there is an area of aspen and mixed forest. 2.7 miles: Open water tank for cattle with a good flow rate. 3.5 miles: Caution—cattle guard. 4.0 miles: You come to a high meadow in a saddle. The road left goes to Haypress Flat—just beyond the trees to the north. 4.9 miles, Start down the ridge. *Caution:* It is steep and dusty. You'll find good shade under the aspen and conifers if you want to stop for a rest.

6.2 miles: You cross a saddle and drop down into a heavily forested area to 6.4 miles where the road comes to a junction with USFS Route 052. The right fork climbs up to State Route 89, the left fork drops down to the Leviathan Mine (see next loop). To complete this loop to Highway 89, climb to the right to a saddle at 6.8 miles where USFS Route 050 comes in from the east. Continue south on the well-graded road to State Highway 89 at mile 8.0. Markleeville is to the right (west), Monitor Pass is to the left (east).

Ride 2   Leviathan Mine Loop

This is a short loop of moderate difficulty with a real feeling of the outback. To start your ride, turn off Highway 89 onto USFS Route 052, 4.8 miles east of State Route 4, and park your car. Ride north on the well-graded dirt road, climbing to a saddle at 1.2 miles. The road to the right is the point you should return to. Stay on the main road dropping down the canyon. At 1.6 miles you pass Route 190 on the left. Continue down to the locked gate and the sign *Private Property* at the Leviathan Mine, mile 2.6. Look for, and follow, the little-used, unmaintained double-track trail that proceeds to the right up the east side of Leviathan Creek. 3.2 miles: Good primitive campsite under huge aspen trees. The trail continues up the canyon to a small meadow and an intersection with a dirt road at 4.1 miles. Go right on Route 050. 5.9 miles: This is the saddle at milepoint 1.2 mentioned above. Turn left to return to Highway 89.

Ride 3   Leviathan Peak Loop

This loop is a classic high plateau traverse which visits some primitive areas with outstanding views. It follows an unmaintained and little-used jeep road which circles the Leviathan Peak Lookout, and is barely a double-track in some spots. It would be considered easy, except for the many lava rocks which require some alertness and dexterity to avoid. Consequently, it is rather slow going. The remoteness and views make it well worth the couple of hours of your time.

From a flat meadow a half mile west of the Monitor Pass marker, take the dirt road leading in a northwesterly direction. Set your odometer to 0.0 at the junction of the dirt road. Cross the meadow, staying to the right as you pass a dry pond and camping site roads leading off into the trees. 0.6 mile: Take the right fork heading uphill. 0.8 mile: Take the left fork. You will be heading due north, following along an old fence line at the 8,400' contour. 2.3 miles: Pass an old water trough to the right with the Lookout Station to the southeast. 2.8 miles: After dropping down into a small meadow, you pass through a small aspen grove. During the fall this track through the grove becomes a golden tunnel! The ground is covered with bright yellow leaves and everything inside the tunnel has an eerie golden glow. It's well worth a trip! The track climbs out to the east at this point to a saddle at 3.2 miles, and you are approximately one airline mile due north of the lookout.

Caution: There is a steep rocky section on the east side of the saddle. Walk your bike around the washouts. At 3.6 miles you come to an intersection. Take the road to the right. 3.8 miles: You pass an old corral and a spring on the left and a pond at 3.9 miles. 4.2 miles: Bear right and return to Highway 89 at 4.7 miles. To return to your starting point, head west to Monitor Pass at 6.3 miles and the starting point at 6.8 miles.

Ride 4   Company Meadows

From the opposite side of the Highway 89 starting point described above, there is a small dirt road that heads out along the Alpine/Mono counties line which makes a good short out and back ride. The road goes due south through a small cut and drops down to an aspen grove and grassy valley, passing a watering pond at 0.75 mile. You can work your way around the old barbed wire fence, keeping to the left side of the fence, and cross the valley to the trees and the ridge farther south.

Ride 5   Indian Springs Road

If you take the road going north opposite the Company Meadows road (083), follow it to its intersection with Road 085, and turn left, you will be travelling north on Indian Springs Road. Begin this ride at the intersection of Highway 88 and Road 085 (see Map 19). Follow Road 085 north until you are in the high flat area just before the area of electronic equipment. At this point you have ridden out of California and into Nevada. If you make a sharp left turn, you will descend rapidly to the springs. Beyond the springs there is opportunity for many miles of exploration! The Indian Springs area shows signs of habitation by Native Americans (obsidian chips and arrowhead fragments) and Basque sheepherders (aspens with signatures and other graffiti). If you turn right just prior to the farthest fenced area, you will be on the service access road for all of this mountaintop equipment. It's a 3.6-mile, rapid downhill to U.S. 395. It comes out 0.7 mile south of the intersection of highways 395 and 208, very near Topaz Lake.

Cooling down on a hot summer day

8 SOUTH LAKE TAHOE

CHAPTER

Paved Bike Trails; Cathedral Road; Angora Lake; Fallen Leaf Road to Glen Alpine Falls; South Lake Tahoe OHV Areas; Twin Peaks Area; Powerline Area; Mr. Toad's Wild Ride

RIDING IN THE TAHOE BASIN   *Map 20 (Area Map)*

The Lake Tahoe Basin Management Unit is the designation given to the National Forest lands surrounding Lake Tahoe. This land used to be a part of the Eldorado, Toiyabe and the Tahoe National Forests. Because of the recreation, development, and land use problems common to the area surrounding the lake, the Management Unit was formed to regulate the use of this unique recreation area. Not all of land surrounding the lake is National Forest land. Some of the land is regulated by state parks (both California and Nevada), and a large portion is private land. This area is promoted heavily as a scenic recreation spot, providing a variety of year-round activities—skiing, snowboarding and snowmobiling in the winter and hiking, biking, boating, fishing, horseback riding in the summer. Because of its popularity and the convenience of numerous hotels, motels and campgrounds, this area can be extremely crowded on the weekends. Unfortunately, due to the incredible numbers of bike riders and tourists, the Lake Tahoe Basin Management Unit has begun to restrict access to mountain bike riders. In addition to the usual Wilderness Area closures (Granite Chief and Desolation Valley) and the Pacific Crest Trail, some of the developed recreation sites are now closed to mountain bike use.

When you arrive in the Lake Tahoe Basin and enter a recreation area, be sure to ask where you can ride. Please don't assume all lands are open unless signed. Up-to-date information about National Forest lands open for riding can be acquired at the Lake Tahoe Visitor Center (located near the turnoff to Fallen Leaf Lake). Ask the U.S. Forest Service for the current handout on bicycling in the Lake Tahoe Basin and the one about off-highway vehicle use. The parts of the Lake Tahoe Basin included in this guidebook are the West Shore as far north as Homewood and the East Shore to the intersection of Highway 28 and U.S. 50. The area to the north is covered in Guide 3B.

Much of the ground surface in the Lake Tahoe Basin is covered with what is called "D.G." (decomposed granite = SAND!). What soil there is, is usually thin. It takes a long time for plants to grow in this area. This is

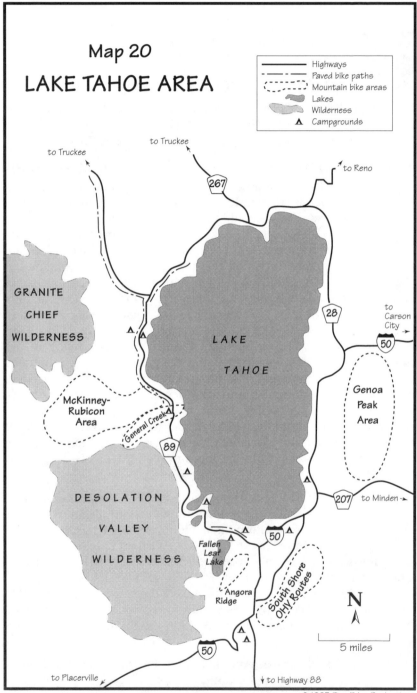

Map 20
LAKE TAHOE AREA

Highways
Paved bike paths
Mountain bike areas
Lakes
Wilderness
▲ Campgrounds

to Truckee

to Truckee

267

to Reno

GRANITE
CHIEF
WILDERNESS

LAKE

TAHOE

28

to Carson City

50

McKinney-Rubicon Area

General Creek

Genoa Peak Area

89

DESOLATION

VALLEY

WILDERNESS

Fallen Leaf Lake

207

to Minden

50

Angora Ridge

South Shore OHV Routes

N

5 miles

50

to Placerville

to Highway 88

© 1993 Fine Edge Productions

a sensitive area! Please stay on the designated routes and don't cut corners or skid your tires! As mentioned in other parts of the book, the Pacific Crest Trail—which runs north-south on the ridge above the West Shore of Lake Tahoe —is now closed statewide to mountain bike use. Another beautiful trail in this area is the Tahoe Rim Trail. This is a 150-mile-long trail, completely encircling the lake, that is being constructed entirely with volunteer effort. At the time of this writing, the Rim Trail is nearly finished and a substantial portion is open to cyclists. To preserve the opportunity for mountain bikers, please use your very best trail etiquette in this area. Later in this book, you will find a map and more information about the Tahoe Rim Trail.

Suggested USFS maps of the area include: Tahoe National Forest Map, Eldorado National Forest Map and the Toiyabe National Forest Map. The current USFS map (1976) titled Lake Tahoe Basin Management Unit is convenient, but very outdated as far as dirt roads available to ride. Also be aware that the Granite Chief Wilderness Map is not on your Tahoe Map. The eastern boundary or the Granite Chief Wilderness Area basically follows the Pacific Crest Trail from Barker Peak north to Squaw Peak. This area is just north of the rides described in Chapter 9.

With this background about the area, we can talk about the great riding it has to offer! Beginners (or those with hybrid or cross bikes) can stick with the flatter ground surrounding Lake Tahoe (mostly on paved bike paths), while the more adventurous should have a great time exploring the high country. Be aware that once you leave the lake every direction is up! The lake level is 6,229', with the surrounding peaks reaching 9,000' and above. Riders from sea level may feel the elevation—you may huff and puff (or choose to walk) up certain sections that at first appear rideable. Carry lots of water, use a sunscreen and check the weather forecast before heading out. The area is known for summer afternoon thundershowers, so be prepared!

As far as the season for riding, it can best be described as *snowmelt to snowfall!* If the ski resorts are still open the dirt riding will be limited (better to read the Pollock Pines and Georgetown Chapters). To be safe consider June through October, but even that will vary with heavy or light snowfall years. Many of the routes in the Lake Tahoe Basin are suitable for winter cross-country ski use. This guide can be helpful for that, too, but remember that things look different in the winter. Many of the trail signs you can see in the summer are buried in the winter. As you ride, be on the lookout for orange or blue diamonds in trees. These are designated winter routes. Also, beware of avalanche hazards!

Riding the high country around the Basin gives you an indication of how big Lake Tahoe really is! This is a beautiful recreation area—a great place for a multi-sport vacation. Hope you enjoy your riding in the Lake Tahoe Basin!

Campgrounds:
1. William Kent Campground. USFS Campground, usually open late May to October 1. No reservations required. 916-573-2600.
2. Kaspian Recreation Area. Small USFS Campground. Open Memorial Day to Labor Day. No reservations. 916-573-2600.
3. General Creek Campground, Sugar Pine Point State Park. Open year-round. Part of the campground has marked trails for cross-country skiing. Showers. Reservations required, call early because this is a very popular park! 916-525-7982. Reservations through Mistix: 1-800-446-PARK.
4. D.L. Bliss State Park. Open during the summer only. Showers. Reservations through Mistix: 1-800-446-PARK. Park phone number: 916-525-7277. This park has lots of Lake Tahoe, Emerald Bay Shoreline to explore!
5. Emerald Bay State Park—same as for D.L. Bliss State Park. Park phone number 916-541-3030.
6. Fallen Leak Campground. Open May 22 to October 1. Reservations recommended. Call Ticketron. Campground phone number 916-544-0426.
7. Camp Richardson. Open mid-May through mid-September. Showers. Call 916-541-1801 for more information.
8. KOA Campground. Located in Meyers on Highway 50. Open April-October 15. Showers. Call 916-577-3693 for more information.
9. Tahoe Pines Campground, located in Meyers on Highway 50. Open May 20 to October 15. Showers. Call 916-577-1653.
10. South Lake Tahoe-El Dorado Campground. Open May through mid-September. Showers. Call 916-573-2059 for more information.
11. Nevada Beach. USFS Campground. No reservations. Open late May to October 1. Call 916-573-2600 for more information.

The above is not a complete list of the campgrounds in the Lake Tahoe Area. These are the closest campgrounds to the rides described in this book. If it says *No Reservations,* this usually means "first-come, first-serve." Try to arrive in the middle of the week to claim a space. Don't drive up late Friday expecting to easily find a place to camp! Due to the popularity of the Lake Tahoe Basin Area, there are very few primitive campsites. If you like to camp outside of campgrounds you are better off camping in the Eldorado, Toiyabe and Tahoe National Forests that surround the Lake Tahoe Area. Don't forget to obtain a campfire permit and find out the current fire conditions.

Bike Shops: There are several bike shops in the South Lake Tahoe Area. If all you need are spare tubes, you can buy them almost anywhere you see bikes out in front of a shop. These are usually bike rental shops which rent everything from kid's BMX bikes, one-speed cruisers to mountain bikes. Be careful if you or your friends plan to rent a bike in the South Lake Tahoe Area. There is a definite difference in quality found at different shops. Test the bike, including the brakes, before leaving the parking lot—be sure the bike you rent is suited for your needs. For better quality rentals, parts for your personal bike, or repairs, check the yellow pages to find full-services bike shops (not just a rental store). There are several located around the shores of Lake Tahoe.

PAVED BIKE TRAILS

Paved bike paths are on the increase in the Lake Tahoe Area. Many of the newer trails are paved pathways where the rider is safely kept away from the busy Lake Tahoe traffic. These bike trails are a great place to get used to your new mountain bike, acclimate to the elevation, ride with your children, tow children in trailers, or just to be a tourist and enjoy the scenery!

Paved trails—quiet riding near the lake

Pope-Baldwin Bike Path

This trail is maintained by the USFS and radiates from the USFS Information Center on the south end of Lake Tahoe. The trail is about 4 miles long. Using this trail, you can ride to Fallen Leaf Lake, Pope and Baldwin Beaches, the Tallac Historical Site, as well as the Visitor's Center. Heading towards the "Y" in South Lake

Tahoe, the trail becomes a bike lane on the side of Highway 89 & U.S. 50.

Tahoma to Tahoe City Bike Path

The southern end of this bike trail begins in Sugar Pine Point State Park and continues northward around Lake Tahoe to Tahoe City, about 10 miles one way. This is a very scenic trail winding through the forest, with sections running right along the shore of Lake Tahoe. Please ride cautiously (especially with children), the trail crosses several side streets and Highway 89 a couple of times.

Tahoe City to Truckee

Starting from Tahoe City, the bike trail follows the Truckee River for approximately 4 miles. After that the path switches to a bike lane along the side of Highway 89. A fun way to use this section of paved trail is to ride the dirt from Tahoe City up over the ridge, down to Truckee, then cruise back on the bike path and take a swim in the Truckee River.

CATHEDRAL ROAD

Going east from the "Y" in South Lake Tahoe (just over 3.5 miles) and just past the Visitors Center, turn left onto Cathedral Road. This route is a 2.8-mile-long access road to an area of private homes on the west side of Fallen Leaf Lake. The first 2.5 miles are a delightful spin through the forest, before you encounter private property covered with cabins. The turnaround is where the road ends at a trailhead for Mt. Tallac. Bikes are legal from here, but the terrain becomes very difficult for cycling.

ANGORA/FALLEN LEAF AREA   *Map 21*

Angora Lake

Topo Maps: 7.5 min. Echo Lake; 15 min. Fallen Leaf. Start: T12N, R18E, section 7.
Mileage: 8 miles round trip; 11 miles from the campground.
Level of Difficulty: Easy.
Water: At the campgrounds in the Basin and at Angora Lake.
Elevation Gain: 1,200' from Fallen Leaf Lake.
Season: June through October.

This is a fun ride, especially if you are staying in the Fallen Leaf or Camp Richardson areas. You can start right from your campsite.

The Drive: Go north on Highway 89 along the southwest side of Lake

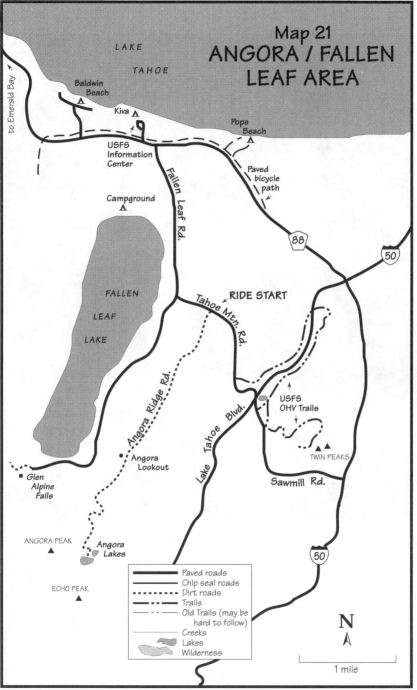

Map 21
ANGORA / FALLEN
LEAF AREA

LAKE TAHOE

Baldwin Beach

Kiva

Pope Beach

to Emerald Bay

USFS Information Center

Paved bicycle path

Campground

Fallen Leaf Rd.

88

50

RIDE START

Tahoe Mtn. Rd.

FALLEN LEAF LAKE

Angora Ridge Rd.

Lake Tahoe Blvd.

USFS OHV Trails

Angora Lookout

TWIN PEAKS

Glen Alpine Falls

Sawmill Rd.

50

ANGORA PEAK

Angora Lakes

ECHO PEAK

	Paved roads
	Chip seal roads
	Dirt roads
	Trails
	Old Trails (may be hard to follow)
	Creeks
	Lakes
	Wilderness

N

1 mile

© 1993 Fine Edge Productions

Glen Alpine Falls

Tahoe, one mile past Camp Richardson to the road to Fallen Leaf Lake. Turn left and go past Fallen Leaf Campground. At a little over 1.75 miles, turn left on a paved road that goes uphill. After 0.4 mile, turn right on the dirt road. There is parking for several cars along the road just before you turn on Road 1214. If you have a larger group, park back by Fallen Leaf Campground.

The Ride: This is an easy ride to follow, just stay on Angora Ridge Road. (Some sections of the road are paved.) After a bit of a climb (600'), you come be out on Angora Ridge with a spectacular view in all directions. 1.5 miles out, you reach the old Angora Lookout. Take a topo map with you so you can recognize the surrounding peaks—Mt. Tallac and Angora Peak, then look down on Fallen Leaf Lake. When you are ready, continue to Angora Lakes. 1.4 miles: The road arrives at a large parking lot and a gate. This is the end of the road for motor vehicles. Check the sign. Hikers, horseback riders and mountain bikes are all still allowed on the trail (an old road) to the lakes. There's plenty of room for everyone, but be sure to watch out for hikers and horseback riders!

The lower lakes are quieter, with most of the hikers heading to the upper lake. If you ride to the upper lake, be prepared to park your bike. The resort owners have built a log bike rack, complete with locks and chains. Lock your bike, then go to the resort and give them your name and the number of your lock. The idea is to provide a safe place to park our bikes and to keep the bikes off the beach area. The resort sells lemonade, ice cream and candy bars and rents small rowboats, so you can take a "cruise" on the lake. Swimming is good here, too. From here, follow your tracks back to your car. *Stay in control at all times and watch out for hikers! Then watch out for vehicles when you reach the road.*

Fallen Leaf Road to Glen Alpine Falls

Although this ride is crowded with mountain bikers most of the summer, it is entirely on pavement. It is a pleasant, relatively flat ride along a beautiful lake, with a spectacular waterfall at the turnaround! The beginning point is at the intersection of Highway 89 and Fallen Leaf Lake Road. You can park at the USFS Information Center (just west of the intersection) or just after turning onto Fallen Leaf Lake Road (alongside the road). Ride south past the campground (at 0.5 mile). At just under 2 miles you pass Tahoe Mountain Road (the road going uphill left past the orange pole gate). At 4.5 miles ride past the marina; 0.2 mile later bear left at the "Y" and follow the sign to Glen Alpine Falls. At 5.0 miles prepare to be impressed—pause a while to enjoy the beautiful waterfalls! This is an out-and-back ride. When you return to your car, the total distance is 10 miles.

South Lake Tahoe OHV Areas

Within the South Shore Area, there are two OHV (Off-Highway Vehicle) Recreational Trails Areas. If you are looking for rides in this area that are not as crowded as the bike paths, give these a try. OHV Trails don't always have the beautiful vista points that other trails in the Tahoe Area have to offer, and they tend to be more technical because they are designed for motor powered use. In other words, they can be a good workout. If you plan to ride in this area, be sure to stop at the Forest Service Information Center by the turnoff for Fallen Leaf Lake and ask for an OHV handout. Look for the South Shore Area, and you will find the two areas described below. Trail work is continuing for the South Shore areas, so you may find more trails than are described here.

Twin Peaks Area

This area is located on Sawmill Road just off Highway 50. Travelling north on Highway 50, two miles from Meyers turn left on Sawmill Road. Continue on Sawmill Road 1.5 miles to where it intersects with Lake Tahoe Boulevard. The Twin Peaks Area is located to the right, heading towards the Twin Peaks. There is a fishing pond on the corner. Turn on the road to the pond, and you will find plenty of parking. This area probably won't be too enjoyable for most recreational riders, except for those who ride to get a workout. The ground surface is predominantly decomposed granite = sand! If it hasn't rained in a while the going can be tough. As far as what to ride, there are basically two loop rides. One takes you to the sand pit and back. The other road, marked 12N14Y, is a loop towards Twin Peaks. There isn't a lot of riding here, but the Twin Peaks Area is important to remember if you are staying in Tahoe and want to get away from the crowds. You can easily ride here from all the motels in the area.

Powerline Area

Topo Maps: 7.5 min. Freel Peak; 15 min. Freel Peak.
Mileage: Round trip from Oneida Street, Fountain Place is approximately 9 miles; Mr. Toad's 4 miles; Hell Hole 8 miles.
Water: Several streams are located in the area; filter or treat all water.

From Highway 50 in Meyers, turn right at the stop signal on Pioneer Trail. Continue on Pioneer Trail 0.9 mile to Oneida Street. Stay on Oneida Street until the road ends at an OHV sign. From here, Oneida Street becomes Forest Road, 12N01, also known as the Fountain Place Road. 12N01 is not much of an OHV route, because it is now chip-sealed all the way up the ridge to the private land at the Fountain Place. To orient yourself, you may want to drive or ride up road 12N01 (with some effort you can connect with the Tahoe Rim Trail to the east). It is steep and narrow, but paved. Radiating from 12N01 are plenty of trails, and up near the top you can ride out another dirt road, 12N01A, towards Hell Hole Meadows. Down at the bottom is Powerline Road, also known as 12N08Y. From 12N01 (Fountain Place Road), turn left on 12N16Y, which goes to 12N08Y. The powerline road is an excellent training road—one short section (just south of High Meadows Trail) has been dubbed "Best Little Downhill West of the Mississippi" by local riders. Note: When exploring this area, be alert to road closures due to private property—respect all signs, gates, and fences.

Mr. Toad's Wild Ride

Total Mileage: 22 miles.
Level of Difficulty: Advanced riders with good singletrack skills.

The Ride: Park in Meyers just off Highway 50 or along Highway 89. Begin by riding south on Highway 89 for 9 miles to the Tahoe Rim Trail parking area on the north side of the road. Ride up the Tahoe Rim Trail to the ridge. The trail is steep and you may have to push your bike at times. 4.5 miles: Once on the ridge, the Tahoe Rim Trail heads right (southeast) to Freel Meadow. For Mr. Toad's Wild Ride, however, turn left (north) and ride through Tucker Flats. Then be prepared for the wild descent. It is a steep, technical downhill that some may prefer to walk in places. The downhill ends on Forest Road 12N02, which turns into Onieda Street. Then turn left onto Pioneer Trail and ride back to your car in Meyers. *Note:* You may find yourself on another OHV Trail and end up in a subdivision. If so, keep riding north and west (to your left) and you will end up in Meyers, where you started the ride.

The tranquil shores of Lake Tahoe on a stormy day

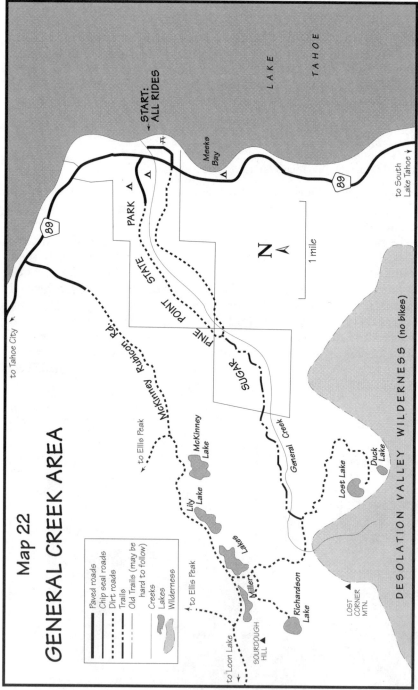

Map 22
GENERAL CREEK AREA

Paved roads
Chip seal roads
Dirt roads
Trails
Old Trails (may be hard to follow)
Creeks
Lakes
Wilderness

START: ALL RIDES

LAKE TAHOE

Meeks Bay

to Tahoe City

to South Lake Tahoe

89

89

N

1 mile

McKinney Rd.

Rubicon Rd.

to Ellis Peak

PARK

STATE

PINE POINT

SUGAR

General Creek

McKinney Lake

Lily Lake

Lakes

Miller Lakes

Richardson Lake

to Ellis Peak

to Loon Lake

SOURDOUGH HILL

Lost Lake

Duck Lake

LOST CORNER MTN.

DESOLATION VALLEY WILDERNESS (no bikes)

© 1993 Fine Edge Productions

9 WEST SHORE LAKE TAHOE

General Creek Loop; Lost Lake; General Creek to McKinney Creek; Barker Pass; Ellis Peak Loop; Rubicon Springs

GENERAL CREEK AREA *Map 22*

The Drive: These rides begin and end at Sugar Pine Point State Park on the West Shore of Lake Tahoe (just over 18 miles from the "Y" in South Lake Tahoe). For a $3 day-use fee you can park inside the park at the picnic area on the east side of Highway 89, or drive into General Creek Campground and park in the day-use lot. General Creek Campground is a wonderful campground to stay in if you are planning a multi-day trip to the Tahoe Area. If you parked in the picnic area, locate the bike path and ride over to the campground to begin the rides.

Ride 1 General Creek Loop

Maps: Start at T14N, R16E, section 20.
Mileage: 6 miles.
Level of Difficulty: Easy—good introduction to mountain bike riding.

The Ride: Ride through the campground following the signs and look for spaces 149-151. The fire road/hiking trail starts from there. 2.5 miles: Turn left, following the loop trail sign. This next section is narrow, so watch for hikers. After crossing the bridge, the trail widens into a fire road again. 1.5 miles: You reach another loop trail marker. For a shorter loop, turn left and you will end up back in the campground. For a longer loop continue straight ahead on the fire road. Within one mile the road dead-ends at Highway 89 just across from the picnic area. Be careful crossing the highway. Then turn left and either ride on the shoulder of Highway 89, or go into the picnic area and take the bike path back to the campground.

Ride 2 Lost Lake

Maps: 7.5 min. Homewood, Rockbound Valley. Warning: The jeep road to Lost Lake is not marked correctly on any of the topo or Forest Service maps.
Mileage: 14 miles.
Level of Difficulty: Intermediate or better riders.
Water: Campground at General Creek at 4.5 miles and Lost Lake at 7 miles.
Seasons: When the snow melts! June 1 to October 30.

— 103 —

Forest cruise

The Ride: Follow the loop ride for the first 2.5 miles. Instead of turning left, continue straight ahead. The single track begins here. 0.5 mile: Turn left, following the sign to Lost Lake. The next 1.5 miles is good, fun trail riding with a bit of rock picking and a few small technical spots. 0.5 mile: This section is rough, with several steep loose sections composed of "D.G." (decomposed granite = SAND). Most people will be on and off their bikes, pushing up to where the trail crosses General Creek. You have now travelled approximately 4.5 miles. Cross the creek, then look carefully for the trail that goes uphill right along the creek. If you are low on water, be sure to refill your water bottles here. *(Be sure to filter or treat all water!)* The rest of the way to Lost Lake is all uphill. Follow the trail. This next section will probably be a push for most people. 0.4 mile: The trail dead-ends into a jeep road. Take a good look around where this trail takes off because it can be hard to locate on your way back down. A right turn here takes you to Miller Lake and the Rubicon Jeep Trail (see Ride 3). Go left here to continue on to Lost Lake.

After riding a short distance the road goes uphill steeply through a boulder washout. After pushing your bike through the rocks, the jeep road is mostly all rideable to the top of the ridge. When you reach the top of the ridge (7,600') the road turns west. Soon, you can see Duck Lake off to your left. After all the climbing you may be tempted to stop here, but Lost Lake is much nicer. Follow the road 0.3 mile to where it ends on a peninsula at Lost Lake. Have lunch, go for a swim, then prepare for a rapid descent back down to General Creek. Don't forget the technical sections and watch for the trails back to the creek. Cross the creek and turn right on the trail back to the park. Follow the trail back to the State Park.

Ride 3   General Creek to McKinney Creek

Topo Maps: 7.5 min. Homewood.
Mileage: 16 miles total.
Level of Difficulty: Intermediate to advanced.
Water: General Creek, Sugar Pine Point State Park.

This is a loop ride which can be done in both directions. The description below takes you in a clockwise direction from the General Creek Campground up to the McKinney-Rubicon Road to Tahoma, where you take the bike path back to the campground.

Follow the Lost Lake Ride to the jeep road (5 miles). Turn right on the

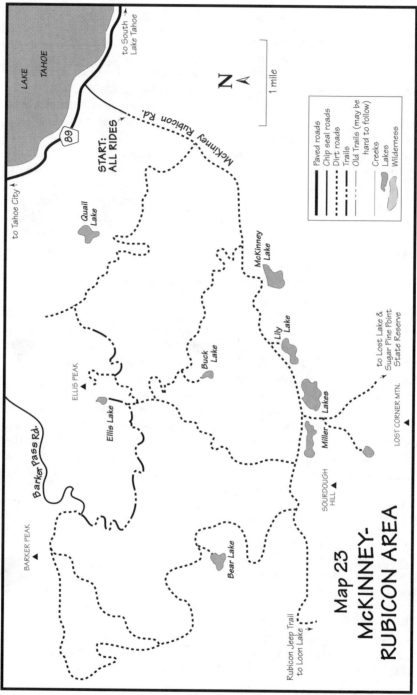

Map 23
McKinney-
RUBICON AREA

LAKE
TAHOE

to South
Lake Tahoe

to Tahoe City

89

START:
ALL RIDES

McKinney Rubicon Rd.

N

1 mile

Paved roads
Chip seal roads
Dirt roads
Trails
Old Trails (may be hard to follow)
Creeks
Lakes
Wilderness

Quail
Lake

McKinney
Lake

Lily
Lake

Buck
Lake

to Lost Lake &
Sugar Pine Point
State Reserve

ELLIS PEAK

Ellis Lake

Miller Lakes

LOST CORNER MTN.

Barker Pass Rd.

SOURDOUGH
HILL

BARKER PEAK

Bear Lake

Rubicon Jeep Trail
to Loon Lake

© 1993 Fine Edge Productions

jeep road. You cross General Creek and then climb the ridge. The rocky peak to the west is Lost Corner Mountain and the edge of Desolation Valley Wilderness Area. After one mile you reach the top of the ridge and begin a gradual descent down the other side. Look off to your right and you should see an old log cabin. Continue on the main road to Miller Lake. When the road ends at Miller Lake turn right on the Rubicon Jeep Trail. The ride continues past Miller Lake, Lily Lake and McKinney Lake. This road is known for the boulder fields you encounter. At first glance, they appear unrideable, but usually there has been enough jeep traffic to pack them together like a very rough cobble road. At 4.4 miles the pavement ends in a subdivision of Tahoma. Turn right on McKinney-Rubicon Road. Turn left on Springs Road, right on Bellvue, then turn left on McKinney-Rubicon Springs Road which ends at Highway 89 in Tahoma. Turn right on the bike trail that runs beside Highway 89 and ride one mile back to Sugar Pine Point State Park.

MCKINNEY-RUBICON AREA   *Map 23*

These rides begin from the town of Tahoma on the West Shore of Lake Tahoe. The dirt roads and trail rides radiate from the McKinney-Rubicon Springs Road, also known as the Rubicon Jeep Trail. This is an extremely popular OHV area. The Rubicon Jeep Trail is an incredibly scenic high country jeep route that connects with the west side of the Sierra at Wentworth Springs (see McKinstry Lake Ride, Chapter 4), travels across the crest along the edge of Desolation Wilderness and ends in Tahoma. This route is rough and rocky with many granite slabs to ride. You can ride a mountain bike from Loon Lake across to Tahoma in a long day's ride. Be prepared to portage around some of the rough sections, but the majority of the road is rideable.

Note: If you are planning on riding all the way across, due to the roughness of the ride it is more fun to do it in a day, travelling light, rather than a multi-days tour with gear. The rides in this section include 5.5 miles of the Rubicon Jeep Trail, then the route turns onto other roads.

The Drive: From the town of Tahoma, go west on McKinney-Rubicon Springs Road (located just south of Chambers Lodge) and follow the signs for McKinney/Rubicon OHV Access. Turn left on Bellvue. Turn right on Springs Road (signed *To Miller Lake*). Then turn left on McKinney-Rubicon. When the road turns to dirt, look for a place to park.

Ride 1   Barker Pass

Topo Maps: 7.5 min. Homewood.
Mileage: 22 miles.
Water: 10 miles at Barker Creek. Most of the lakes in this area are covered with lilies, so rely on streams for water. If it is a hot, dry August don't pass up a stream thinking there may be water farther on.
Elevation: 6,230'–8,740'.
Seasons: June 1 through October 30.
Level of Difficulty: Advanced riders only. If you are from sea level, the elevation may get to you when you're riding in the Lake Tahoe Basin Area. From the Basin, up is the only direction the trails go. Most of the rides have at least 1,000' of climbing with climbs of 2,500' not uncommon.

The Ride: Continue on the McKinney-Rubicon Road on your bike. The road is known for its boulder creek crossings, most of which are dry by August. The boulders are impressive, stacked together by years of 4-wheel drive traffic. Riders not used to riding the rocks may think these sections are unrideable, but if you find the right gear (low, but not *too* low!), get up off the saddle and keep the pedals spinning, you can ride through them all. 0.7 mile: Look off to your right for a side road that crosses a bridge. If you ride the Ellis Peak Loop this is where you'll come out. Continue straight ahead. 1.3 miles: Continue on the main road to

Bridge break

Miller Lakes. (The 4-wheel drive road to the right climbs to Buck Lake, then on up to Ellis Peak. We have ridden UP this road once. It climbs 900' in 1.2 miles, often through rocky sections. We probably pushed as much as we rode the first part of this road. If you choose to come down this one, use caution. This route is technical in *both* directions!)

1.2 miles: Off to your left is the first in a series of lakes—McKinney Lake. Next you'll pass Lily Lake, then Upper and Lower Miller Lakes. This series of lakes are full of lily pads. 2 miles: Just as you pass Lower Miller Lake, you'll see a road to the left. This road goes to Richardson Lake, Lost Lake and Sugar Pine Point State Park. (For loop rides in this direction, see Rides 2 & 3, General Creek Area.) Continue straight ahead. 0.6 mile: Just past Upper Miller Lake, another jeep road enters from the right. It is a steep climb to Ellis Peak (Buck Lake Road joins this one). This is one of those roads that's a scream to come down and a definite workout in the uphill direction! Continue on past this road for the longer loops.

A half mile farther, the road splits (to the left is the Rubicon Trail that goes to Rubicon Springs and Loon Lake). Go to the right on the road to Barker Pass. The first mile is all up, on a good dirt surface. After climbing to the top of the ridge, you descend towards Bear Lake. Then the road circles the lake and continues. There are roads all through this section— just remember to stay on the main road unless you want to go exploring! At 4.0 miles you leave the lake and climb some more. If you look carefully you should see where the Pacific Crest Trail crosses the road. 0.4 mile farther on, you cross Barker Creek. The main road continues straight ahead, winds around, gradually climbing, then eventually reach Barker Pass. The jeep road to the right (just after you cross the creek) is a short cut to the top. The jeep road follows Barker Creek, goes along the edge of Barker Meadows, then takes you past "Red Cabin Estates," an old cabin in great condition, painted bright red! Continue on the main road that suddenly starts climbing. Like most short cuts, it is steeper, but it's a much quicker route to Barker Pass. If you choose the road up Barker Creek, you will be riding through private land. *Be sure to stay on the road; no camping allowed.*

2 miles (on the short cut), 3.5 miles (on the main road): Both roads meet at the top of Barker Pass. This is a great spot to enjoy the view in all directions. Take a rest, refuel and get ready for a bit of pushing! When you are ready to go, turn right (east) on Barker Pass Road. 0.5 mile: Just as the road changes from dirt to pavement, look to your right and you'll see the motorcycle/hiking trail. The trail climbs 600' in about seven

switchbacks, some of which is rideable, but if it hasn't rained in a while the soil will be loose and most people will push the first part. The view from the next stretch of trail is spectacular! To the southwest you can see Loon Lake (the biggest lake) and the rocky terrain of Desolation Valley Wilderness Area. To the northwest are Blackwood Canyon and Lake Tahoe. After some fun, single-track downhill, the trail begins to climb again towards the top of Ellis Peak. 2 miles: The trails ends at a sign indicating Ellis *Lake [left]*. A left here takes you to Ellis Lake 0.4 mile. Go right to continue the loop. 0.3 mile: The road splits.

Continue straight ahead. (This may happen anyway if you are rapidly descending.) The next 3 miles is a fast descent with one rest spot when you reach a large meadow at North Miller Creek. This road drops from 8,200' to Miller Meadows at 7,100' in three miles—most of the drop in the last 1.5 miles! Be *careful. Some of the steep sections are loose and rocky.* The road ends at McKinney Road. Turn left and enjoy 5 more miles of downhill back to your car. Watch out for the boulder patches, they actually seem rougher on the way down than on the way up! *Total mileage Route A: 22.5 miles.*

Ride 2   Ellis Peak Loop

Ellis Peak Loop was the 1988 Tahoe-Roubaix race course. The Tahoe-Roubaix is one of the most challenging and scenic rides held in the Sierra.

The Ride: Follow Barker Pass Loop for the first 15 miles to the Ellis Lake Intersection, turn right; then after a short 0.2 mile, take a sharp left to finish the climb to Ellis Peak. 0.3 mile: The road splits. If you look to the left you'll see the rocky top of Ellis Peak. If you are out to enjoy the scenery, go left. Ride the last pitch as far as possible. Then park your bike and climb to the top of Ellis Peak, elevation 8,740'. Enjoy the 360° view. Ride back down to where the road splits and continue on the jeep road. As the road leaves the ridge, stay to the left and the road becomes a single-track trail through the forest. When the single-track ties back into a jeep road, go left (actually straight ahead). 1.5 miles: After more descending, go right on the dirt road. This road contours around the ridge, crosses Homewood Creek, then turns the corner for yet another great view of Lake Tahoe, this time looking down on Quail Lake and Homewood Ski Area. *This section of the road passes through private land, so stay on the road at all times.* After enjoying the view, prepare for the last 3 miles of wild downhill on the Noonchester Mine Road. *Stay in control and always be ready for uphill traffic.* When you reach the bottom, cross the creek and turn left on McKinney Road to return to your car.

Ride 3   Rubicon Springs

Topo Maps: 7.5 min. Homewood, Wentworth Springs, Loon Lake.
Mileage: 19 miles total.
Level of Difficulty: Advanced—challenging ride for those who enjoy rough,
rocky, technical terrain.
Elevation: 6,063'–7,100'. The elevation gain on this ride is a bit deceiving
because you gain 900', then lose 1,100' on the way out, so you must gain
1,100' to lose the final 900'!

The Ride: Follow the Barker Pass Loop (Ride 1) to where the road to Bear
Lake heads north to Barker Pass, 5.5 miles out. Continue straight ahead
on the Rubicon Jeep Trail. The road continues westward not far from
Miller Creek then turns north and begins descending. From here, the
riding gets rougher when you get out on the granite rocks, then the trail
turns southward and drops 700' in about a mile down to the Rubicon
River. The road mellows out as you follow the Rubicon River upstream
to Rubicon Springs 4 miles. The area around Rubicon Springs is private
land. This is the spot where big parties take place during the Jeepers
Jamboree, a group jeep ride held every summer on the Rubicon Trail. A
band is flown in by helicopter and a full mechanics shop set up to try
to repair any major damage done to the jeeps on the trail. It's a pretty
site located along the Rubicon River and surprisingly clean considering
the large numbers of groups that travel through at one time. The biggest
shock is the number of outhouses in one small area. *Due to the number
of outhouses located close to the stream, I wouldn't recommend filling water
bottles near this area.*

You could continue your ride westward towards Loon Lake or Wentworth
Springs, approximately 10 miles farther. It's an enjoyable ride for those
who don't mind pushing. A great way to do this ride is to arrange a
shuttle and ride one-way only, about 20 miles. If 40 miles does not sound
like much, be advised that this is ROUGH, ROCKY COUNTRY! When you
have finished exploring at Rubicon Springs, get ready for the climb up
out of the canyon back to Miller Lakes, then on back to Tahoe.

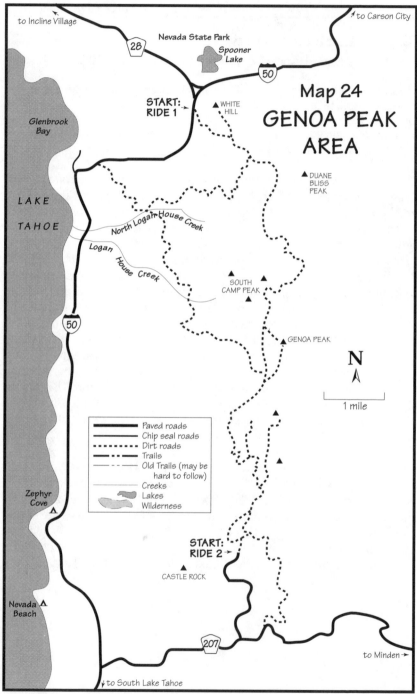

to Incline Village

to Carson City

28

Nevada State Park

Spooner Lake

50

START: RIDE 1

▲ WHITE HILL

Map 24
GENOA PEAK
AREA

Glenbrook Bay

▲ DUANE BLISS PEAK

LAKE

TAHOE

North Logan House Creek

Logan House Creek

▲ SOUTH CAMP PEAK
▲

▲ GENOA PEAK

N

50

1 mile

	Paved roads
	Chip seal roads
	Dirt roads
	Trails
	Old Trails (may be hard to follow)
	Creeks
	Lakes
	Wilderness

Zephyr Cove ⚲

START: RIDE 2

▲ CASTLE ROCK

Nevada ⚲ Beach

207

to Minden

to South Lake Tahoe

© 1993 Fine Edge Productions

10 EAST SHORE LAKE TAHOE

South Camp Loop; Kingsbury to Spooner; Tahoe Rim Trail

GENOA PEAK AREA *Map 24*

One of the OHV areas suggested by the Lake Tahoe Basin Management Unit is the Genoa Peak Area, located on the East Shore of Lake Tahoe. This area runs north and south up on the ridges between Spooner Summit and Kingsbury Grade. Neither side could be considered as beginner riding—the elevation losses and gains happen quickly in both directions. In the southern access, the road surface is mostly "D.G." (decomposed granite = SAND), with not too much shade. The heat from the reflection can be intense on a hot summer day. There is no water on the southern side. The northern access from Spooner Summit is much more forested. We explored this area (both north and south) in the August heat of the 1988 drought, and Logan House Creek was still running cold and clear enough so we could filter water. All the other creeks shown on the USGS maps were dry. This area is marked all the way across with orange diamonds for snowmobile and cross-country ski use.

South Camp Loop

Topo Maps: 7.5 min. Glenbrook (Nevada). Start: T14N, R18E, section 12.
Mileage: 16.5 miles total.
Water: Logan House Creek. Filter or treat all water.
Level of Difficulty: Strenuous intermediate to advanced ride. The road surface is all pretty straight forward 4-wheel drive road with only about a mile of rocky uphill. With 1,700' of climbing in the beginning and another 500' gain later on, this ride will feel longer than the 16 miles.
Season: Mid-May through October.

The South Camp Loop takes you through several large aspen groves, making this a fantastic fall color ride. The most scenic time to do the ride is probably just after the first freeze, some time in mid-October, when the aspens turn from shiny green to bright yellow and orange. If you choose to ride in the fall, be prepared for that first snowfall of the season. Dress in layers, carry tights and a windbreaker.

The Drive: From South Lake Tahoe continue east on U.S. 50 past the casinos continuing on up the East Shore of Lake Tahoe. Stay on U.S. 50

The Tahoe area offers cyclists world-class rest stops.

to Spooner Junction where Highway 28 intersects with 50. Look on the southeast side of the road for the highway maintenance station and turn in here. Park out of the way near the maintenance station. Please be aware that the nearby section of the Tahoe Rim Trail (and the route from Spooner Lake area to Genoa Peak) is closed to mountain bikes. The Forest Service has made that closure because Genoa Peak Road is nearby and basically covers the same territory.

The Ride: Consider riding back and forth on the flats along the highway before starting. Try to stretch and loosen up a bit because this ride goes up right away. After loosening up, ride out the road behind the maintenance station, Genoa Peak Road. At 0.9 mile stay right on Genoa Peak Road (road to the left climbs to the top of White Hill and dead-ends. At 0.6 mile is where the loop begins and ends. This ride can be done in either direction with good ups and downs either way. These directions continue clockwise. Stay left on the road marked 14N32. 1.8 miles: At this intersection, you may want to go left a short distance to the overlook where the mountains drop straight down to the Carson Valley. After taking a look, go right at this intersection.

The road continues to climb gradually at first, then the road surface turns to loose rock and gets much steeper. If it's not too torn up and you have the determination, it's all rideable, though you may choose to walk certain sections. When you reach the switchback the climb is almost over. 0.8 mile: You top out on the ridge of South Camp Peak 8,700'. (South Camp Peak is a large plateau with three peaks rising up from the flat.) Continue left on the main road. Then it's time for the downhill to begin. 1.5 miles: This is the southernmost point of the ride; go right to follow the loop. If you continue straight ahead the road leads to Kingsbury Grade (4 miles of dirt, then 2 miles of pavement). If you start to climb again you missed this turn!

2.8 miles: Logan House Creek! A small creek in a shady aspen grove. This creek was the only creek on this ride still running in September during the drought of 1988. Be sure to filter or treat all water. Continue on for some more winding downhill with lots of waterbars. 1.8 miles: You cross North Logan House Creek (dry by the end of summer). Turn right to finish the loop. The last climb snakes through a meadow, then winds its way back up to the top of the ridge. The next section contours around Montreal Canyon and then climbs to the top. At 2.4 miles, stay right on the main road. It is 0.4 mile back to the intersection of Genoa Peak Road. Go left and enjoy the last downhill back to your car.

Kingsbury to Spooner (or Spooner to Kingsbury)

Topo Maps: 7.5 min. South Lake Tahoe; Glenbrook, Nevada. Start: T13N, R19E, section 18.
Mileage: South Camp Peak Loop 21.5 miles.
Water: Only at Logan House Creek. Treat or filter all water!
Level of Difficulty: Intermediates or better who enjoy climbing and descending!
Elevation: Kingsbury 7,760–8,700'–7,000 Spooner.

These directions will help you locate the southern end of the riding in this area. The ride can be done straight across south to north, or north to south with a shuttle set up, or you can start from the southern end, continue out to Genoa Peak, then add the South Camp Peak Loop to make a 21.5-mile loop ride.

The Drive: Go east on Highway 50 across the State Line. Turn right on Nevada State Route 207 that goes over Kingsbury Grade. Just before reaching the top of Daggett Pass, turn left (north) on North Benjamin. Stay on North Benjamin through the subdivision where the road becomes Andria Drive. Continue until the road turns to dirt. Park here.

The Ride: Starting from this side, there are roads everywhere so pay

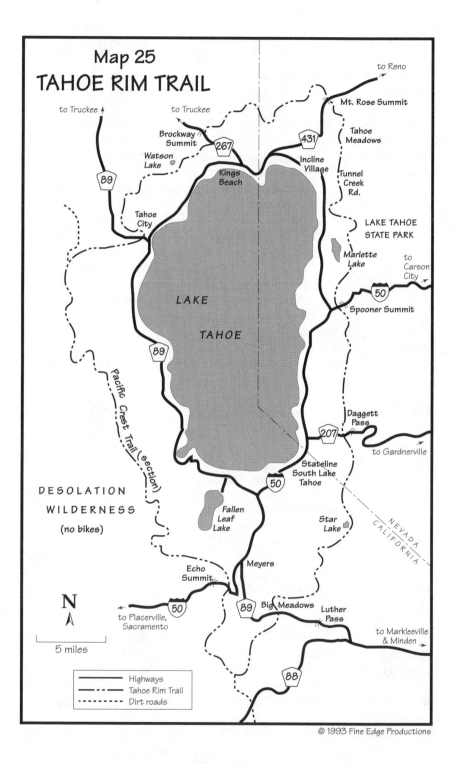

Map 25
TAHOE RIM TRAIL

to Reno
Mt. Rose Summit
to Truckee
to Truckee
Brockway Summit
267
Watson Lake
431
Tahoe Meadows
Kings Beach
Incline Village
Tunnel Creek Rd.
Tahoe City
LAKE TAHOE STATE PARK
Marlette Lake
to Carson City
LAKE
TAHOE
50
Spooner Summit
89
Pacific Crest Trail (section)
Daggett Pass
207
to Gardnerville
DESOLATION
WILDERNESS
(no bikes)
Stateline South Lake Tahoe
50
Fallen Leaf Lake
Star Lake
NEVADA
CALIFORNIA
Echo Summit
Meyers
N
50
89
Big Meadows
Luther Pass
to Placerville, Sacramento
to Markleeville & Minden
5 miles
88

Highways
Tahoe Rim Trail
Dirt roads

© 1993 Fine Edge Productions

attention to the directions. The wrong turns can lead to a lot of steep climbing, great views and dead-ends. The first time we attempted this ride we did 14 miles, gaining and losing several thousand feet in elevation and only rode 3.5 miles in the right direction! The key here is to follow the orange diamonds located in the trees for winter travel. If you go a ways without seeing an orange diamond, go back to the last intersection and scout around a bit.

Go up the main road past the first two roads to the left (0.2 and 0.3 mile). Turn left after a half mile on the third road to the left. 0.4 mile: Turn right uphill. After a short downhill you arrive at a large, flat, open area with trails and track everywhere. Continue straight ahead (a bit to the left). The main fork to the right goes up about 500' then dead-ends on the top of a peak. It is a tough climb, but the view from the top is spectacular! At 0.7 mile you ride through a green gate that is closed in the winter. After 0.6 mile farther, you arrive at a great place to see Lake Tahoe. It is spots like this that give you an idea of just how big this lake really is! Just past the viewpoint, the road forks again. You will feel as if you should continue straight ahead, but don't, this road ends 1.5 miles out. Turn left and just around the corner you should see more orange diamonds with arrows leading you around two hairpin turns.

The road becomes easier to follow now—more orange diamonds and fewer spur road crossings. After a fun descent with the road winding in and out of canyons, there is a 0.6-mile climb to the 8,500' elevation. 0.5 mile (4 miles total): The road splits again. Orange diamonds can be found in both directions. Straight ahead is the main road, Genoa Peak Road, and to the left (west) is the road to Logan House Creek. From this point you can go left towards Logan House Creek (see South Camp Loop Ride 1), or go right on Genoa Peak Road and continue on 7.8 miles to Spooner Summit on Highway 50. Remember, this ride can be done out and back, as a loop, or one way across, with a shuttle. Plan your route before you start the ride.

TAHOE RIM TRAIL   Map 25

The Tahoe Rim Trail is a 150-mile-long hiking, cycling, and equestrian trail that completely encircles Lake Tahoe. The trail is being constructed by volunteers and is financed by donations. Trail building began in 1984 and as of this writing is nearly complete. It passes through six counties in two states (California and Nevada) and incorporates a nearly 50-mile section of the Pacific Crest Trail, which is most of the western portion of the loop. There are numerous steep areas on this trail, with elevations ranging from 6,300' to 9,300'. The Tahoe Rim Trail is marked with blue, triangle-shaped "TRT" signs.

In the summer of 1993, several mountain biking trail signs appeared on parts of the Tahoe Rim Trail. This was the result of a study released by the Forest Service's Lake Tahoe Basin Management Unit. The 34-page document was in response to an ongoing debate between hikers and cyclists regarding the use of this trail. The jury is still out on some portions of the trail. In the south half of the Lake Tahoe area, it is clear that mountain bikes are prohibited on the Pacific Crest Trail and are allowed on the section from Luther Pass (Big Meadows) north to Heavenly Valley ski area (Highway 207). The Big Meadows trailhead is off Highway 89, just over 5 miles southeast of the 50/89 junction in Meyers, where parking, water, and restrooms are available. The Heavenly trailhead is 1.5 miles south of Highway 207 (Kingsbury Grade)—the trail starts one-eighth mile up the "Stagecoach" ski run. This section of trail is about 22 miles one way and is best suited to advanced riders, especially since it is an out-and-back ride.

With time, much more of the Tahoe Rim Trail may become available for mountain biking. In a large part this will depend upon the problems created by combining hikers, horses, and bikes on the already approved sections of this 18-inch-wide trail. Those who oppose cyclists using the Tahoe Rim Trail are most concerned with the issue of speed. If all mountain bikers are courteous and ride under control at all times, we can anticipate that as much as 80 or 90 miles of the trail will be open to cycling. Practice trail etiquette and encourage others cyclists to follow it too!

For more information on the Tahoe Rim Trail or to make a donation of time or money to support the effort, contact the TRT, P.O. Box 10156, South Lake Tahoe, CA 96158.

IMBA Rules of the Trail

Thousands of miles of dirt trails have been closed to Mountain Bicycling because of the irresponsible riding habits of a few riders. Do your part to maintain trail access by observing the following rules of the trail:

1. **Ride on open trails only.** Respect trail and road closures (ask if not sure), avoid possible trespass on private land, obtain permits and authorization as may be required. Federal and State wilderness areas are closed to cycling. Additional trails may be closed because of sensitive environmental concerns or conflicts with other users. Your riding example will determine what is closed to all cyclists!

2. **Leave no trace.** Be sensitive to the dirt beneath you. Even on open trails, you should not ride under conditions where you will leave evidence of your passing, such as on certain soils shortly after a rain. Observe the different types of soils and trail construction; practice low-impact cycling. This also means staying on the trail and not creating any new ones. Be sure to pack out at least as much as you pack in.

3. **Control your bicycle!** Inattention for even a second can cause disaster. Excessive speed maims and threatens people; there is no excuse for it!

4. **Always yield trail.** Make known your approach well in advance. A friendly greeting (or bell) is considerate and works well; startling someone may cause loss of trail access. Show your respect when passing others by slowing to a walk or even stopping. Anticipate that other trail users may be around corners or in blind spots.

5. **Never spook animals.** All animals are startled by an unannounced approach, a sudden movement, or a loud noise. This can be dangerous for you, others, and the animals. Give animals extra room and time to adjust to you. In passing, use special care and follow the directions of horseback riders (ask if uncertain). Running cattle and disturbing wild animals is a serious offense. Leave gates as you found them, or as marked.

6. **Plan ahead.** Know your equipment, your ability, and the area in which you are riding – and prepare accordingly. Be self-sufficient at all times, keep your machine in good repair, and carry necessary supplies for changes in weather or other conditions. A well-executed trip is a satisfaction to you and not a burden or offense to others. Keep trails open by setting an example of responsible cycling for all mountain bicyclists.

APPENDIX B

The Care and Feeding of a Mountain Bike
— *Routine Checkups for Your Bicycle* —

The key to years of fun and fitness from your mountain bike is giving it checkups on a regular basis. You need to know how to clean it, lubricate a few places, make simple adjustments, and recognize when something needs expert attention. For the average rider, most bike shops recommend tune-ups once a year and complete overhauls every two to three years. All of the maintenance in between your trips to the bike shop you can do yourself. Given below is a nine-step checkup procedure, a list to run through after every extensive ride, before you head back out into the hills again.

1. Clean-up
Unless the frame is really filthy, use a soft rag and a non-corrosive wax/polish such as Pledge to wipe off the grime and bring the old shine back. If you need to use water or soap and water prior to the polish, don't high pressure spray directly at any of the bearing areas (pedals, hubs, bottom bracket or head set). You should clean all your components too (including the chain and the rear cogs), but use a different rag and a lubricant such as Tri-Flow or Finish Line for wiping them down. Do not use polish or lubricants to clean your rims—an oily film will reduce your braking ability. Instead, wipe off the rims with a clean dry rag. If you need to remove rubber deposits from the sidewalls of the rims use acetone as a solvent.

2. Inspection
After you get the grit and grime off, check out the frame very carefully, looking for bulges or cracks. If there are chips or scratches that expose bare metal (especially when the metal is steel) use automotive or bicycle touchup paint to cover them up. Your inspection should also include the components. Look for broken, bent or otherwise visibly damaged parts. Pay special attention to the wheels. When you spin them, watch the rim where it passes the brake pads. Look for wobbles and hops, and if there is a lot of movement, the wheel needs to be trued at home (or take it to a bike shop) before using it. Look for loose or broken spokes. And finally, carefully check your tires for sidewall damage, for heavy tread wear, and for cuts and bulges, glass and nails, thorns or whatever.

3. Brakes
Grab the brakes and make sure they don't feel mushy and that the pads are contacting the rim firmly (be certain the brake pads do not rub against the tires!). If the brakes don't feel firm, there are barrel adjusters at one or both ends of the wire cables that control the brakes—turn them counterclockwise to take up some of the slack. If you are unsure as to the dependability of your brakes, for safety's sake let a bike shop check them.

4. Bearing Areas
Most cyclists depend upon professional mechanics to fix any problems in the

pedals, hubs, bottom bracket or head set, but they should be able to recognize when something is wrong. Spin the wheels, spin the crankarms (and the pedals) and move the handlebars from side to side. If you feel notches or grittiness, or if you hear snapping, grating or clicking noises, you have a problem. Check to make sure each of the four areas is properly tightened. To check for looseness try to wiggle a crankarm side to side or try to move a wheel side to side. Check your headset adjustment by holding the front brake, rocking the bike forward and backward and listening for clunking sounds.

5. Shifting

Presuming your bike has gears, check to make sure you can use all of them. The most common problem is the stretching of the inner wire which operates the rear derailleur. If your bike is not shifting properly try turning the barrel adjuster which is located where the cable comes out of the derailleur. Turn it just a little, and usually a counterclockwise direction is what you need. Unless you know what you are doing, avoid turning the little adjustment screws on the derailleurs.

6. Nuts and Bolts

Make sure the nuts and bolts which hold everything together are tight. The handlebars and stem should not move around under pressure, and neither should your saddle. And make certain that the axle nuts or quick releases that hold your wheels are fully secure—when a wheel falls off, the result is almost always crashtime. If you have quick release hubs, they operate as follows: Mostly tighten them by holding the nut and winding the lever, but finish the job by swinging the lever over like a clamp (it's spring loaded). Do not wind them up super tight like you would with a wingnut—for safe operation they must be clamped, and clamped very securely, with considerable spring tension! If you are at all uncertain regarding the use of quick releases, go by a bike shop and ask for a demonstration.

7. Accessories

Make sure all your accessories, from water bottles to bags to pumps to lights, are operational and secure. Systematically check them all out and if you carry flat fixing or other on-the-road repair materials or tools, make sure you've got what you need and you know how to use what you carry. Statistics show that over 90% of all bicycle breakdowns are the result of flat tires, so it is recommended that you carry a pump, a spare tube, a patch kit, and a couple of tire levers with you whenever you ride.

8. Lubrication

The key to long-term mechanical happiness for you and your bike is proper and frequent lubrication. The most important area of lubrication is the chain—spray it with a Teflon-based or other synthetic oil (WD-40, household oil, and motor oil are not recommended), then wipe off all the excess. You can use the same lubricant for very sparsely coating the moving parts of your brakes and derailleurs.

9. Inflation

You now are ready for the last step. Improper inflation can lead to blowouts or pinch flats. Read the side of your tires to see what the recommended pressure is and fill them up. If there is a range of pressures given, use the high figure for street cycling, the low figure or near it for off-road riding. After going through these nine steps of getting your bike ready you've earned another good long ride!

APPENDIX C

Basic Skills for Mountain Biking

Everybody knows how to ride a bike—at least most everybody can ride around the neighborhood. But with the advent of the mountain bike, riding a two-wheel pedal powered machine has gotten more complicated. Watch a pro-level mountain bike race and the need for "technical skills" will become obvious. Can you handle steep hills, big rocks, creeks, muddy bogs, loose sand, big tree roots, deep gravel, or radical washboards? These are the kinds of factors that differentiate mountain biking from road riding and that demand skills and balance above and beyond those required to ride around the neighborhood. The key to acquiring these abilities is practice—start easy and work diligently until you achieve high-level control of your bike.

1. Bicycle

All mountain bikes are not created equal. Some are better suited to staying on pavement. They have too much weight, too long a wheelbase, ineffective braking systems, sloppy shifting, too smooth of tread on the tires, poorly welded frames, and so on. As a general rule, the mountain bicycles marketed by the discount store chains, department stores, and sporting goods stores are only suited to on-road, non-abusive use. Bicycles from bike stores, excepting their least expensive models, are generally suited to heavy duty, skilled off-road use. They should be relatively light (under 30 pounds), and have a fairly short wheelbase and chainstay (for agility), moderately steep head angle (again for agility), strong and dependable braking and shifting systems, well-made frames, and knobby/aggressive tires. For details on choosing the right bike for you, consult the experts at your local bike shop. They can help you not only with selecting a bicycle, but also with various accessory decisions, in such areas as suspension forks, bar ends, and gear ratio changes. And of extreme importance, whatever bike you decide on, get the right size for you. If a bike is too big for your height and weight, no matter how hard you try you will never be able to properly handle it. If you are in doubt or in between sizes, for serious off-road riding opt for the smaller bike.

2. Fundamental Principles

There are some very general rules for off-road riding that apply all the time. The first, "ride in control," is fundamental to everything else. Balance is the key to keeping a bike upright—when you get out of control you will lose your ability to balance the bike (that is, you will crash). Control is directly related to speed and excessive speed for the conditions you are facing is the precursor to loss of control. When in doubt, slow down!

The second principle for off-road riding is "read the trail ahead." In order to have time to react to changes in the trail surface and to obstacles, you should be looking ahead 10 to 15 feet. Especially as your speed increases, you want to avoid being surprised by hazardous trail features (rocks, logs, roots, ruts, and so on)—if you see them well ahead, you can pick a line to miss them, slow down to negotiate them, or even stop to walk over or around them.

The third principle is to "stay easy on the grips." One of the most common reactions by novices in tough terrain is to tense up, most noticeably in a "death grip" on the handlebars. This level of tightness not only leads to hand, arm and shoulder discomfort but interferes with fluid, supple handling of the bike. Grip loosely and bend at the elbows a bit—don't fight the bicycle, work with it!

The last general principle to be presented here is "plan your shifting." If you are looking ahead on the trail, there should be no shifting "surprises." Anticipate hills, especially steep ascents, and shift before your drivetrain comes under a strong load. Mountain bikes have a lot of gears and their proper use will make any excursion more enjoyable.

3. Climbing

Mountain bikes were originally single-speed, balloon-tired cruisers taken by truck or car to the top of a hill and then used for exciting and rapid descent. After a few years, to eliminate the shuttle they were given gears. Today's off-road bikes have 18 to 24 speeds, with a few extremely low gears so they can climb very steep hills. One of the keys to long or difficult climbs is "attitude"—its a mental thing, in that you need to be able to accept an extended, aerobic challenge with the thoughts "I can do it" and "this is fun."

Your bike is made with hill climbing in mind. Find a gear and a pace that is tolerable (not anaerobic) and try to maintain it. Pick a line ahead, stay relaxed, and anticipate shifting, as noted earlier. In addition, be alert to problems in weight distribution that occur when climbing. It is best to stay seated, keeping your weight solidly over the traction (rear) wheel if possible. However, if the slope is so steep that the front wheel lifts off of the ground you will have to lean forward and slide toward the front of the saddle. Constant attention to weight distribution will give you optimum traction and balance for a climb. And make sure your saddle height is positioned so when your foot is at the bottom of a pedal stroke, your knee is very slightly bent—a saddle too low or too high will significantly reduce both power and control on a steep and difficult climb.

4. Descending

This is where most serious accidents occur, primarily because a downhill lends itself to high speed. It is unquestionably the most exciting part of mountain bike riding— expert riders reach speeds up to 60 mph! For descents, the "stay in control" and "read the trail ahead" principles can be injury- saving. Know your ability and don't exceed it. And be certain your brakes are in good working order—don't believe the slogan "brakes are for sissies"—on steep and difficult downhills everyone has to use them. Regarding braking, always apply the rear brake before the front (to avoid an "endo," that is, flying over the handlebars), and if possible, brake in spurts rather than "dragging" them. On easy hills, practice using your brakes to get comfortable with them.

As was the case for steep uphills, steep descents require attention to weight distribution. Many riders lower their saddle an inch or two prior to descending (to get a lower center of gravity). All cyclists quickly learn to lift their weight slightly off the saddle and shift it back a few inches to keep traction and to avoid the feeling of being on the verge of catapulting over the handlebars—practice this weight transfer on smooth but steep downhills so you can do it comfortably later on obstacle-laden terrain. Finally, it is possible to go too slow on a difficult downhill, so slow you can't "blast" over obstacles. Instead, because of lack of momentum, hazards can bring you to an abrupt stop or twist your front wheel, and both of these results can cause loss of control.

5. Turning

A particularly treacherous time for mountain bikers is high speed or obstacle-laden turns. The first principle is don't enter a curve too fast. Turns often contain loose dirt and debris created by all the mountain bikes that preceded you. Slow down before you get to it; you can always accelerate during the turn if you choose. Lean around the turn as smoothly as possible, always keeping an eye out for obstacles. It is common for the rear wheel to skid in turns. To take the fright out of that phenomenon, go find a gentle turn with soft dirt and practice skidding to learn how you and your bike will respond.

6. Obstacles

If you get into the real spirit of off-road cycling, you will not ride just on smooth, groomed trails. You will encounter rocks, roots, limbs, logs, trenches, ruts, washboards, loose sand (or dirt or gravel), and water in a variety of forms from snow and ice to mud bogs to free-flowing springs and creeks.

Obviously, the easiest means for handling an obstacle is to go around it; however, you can't always do that. For raised obstacles, those you need to get up and over, riders need to learn to "pop the front wheel." To practice this, find a low curb or set out a 4x4 piece of lumber. Approach it, and just before the front wheel impacts it, rapidly push down then pull up the front wheel. The wheel lift is enhanced if you simultaneously lower and raise your torso and apply a hard pedal stroke. After your front wheel clears the obstacle, shift your weight up and forward a little so the rear wheel can bounce over it lightly.

If you encounter "washboards," the key to relatively painless negotiating is to maintain a moderate speed and get into a shock absorbing posture—slightly up and off the saddle, knees slightly bent, elbows slightly bent, loose grip on the handlebars, and relaxed. Soft spots in the trail can make your bike difficult to control and create an instant slowdown. If you have to deal with loose, deep sand, dirt or gravel, the key is to go slower but "power through." Shift your weight back a little (for better traction), then keep your bike straight and keep pedaling. Maintaining momentum and a straight line is also important in mud holes, and be certain to do any shifting prior to soft spots or muddy bogs (otherwise you will lose momentum). Sharp turns can present a particular problem in these conditions—you will be much more prone to losing the rear wheel to a slide out, so be extra cautious in sandy or muddy curves.

Going through water can be a lot of fun, or it can be a rude awakening if you end up upside-down on a cold February afternoon. Before any attempt to cross a waterway, stop and examine it first. Make sure it isn't so deep that it will abruptly stop you, then find the route that has the least obstacles (look for deep holes, big rocks, and deep sand). Approach the crossing at a fairly low speed and plan on pedaling through it (rather than coasting) for maximum traction and control. Be aware of the potential for harmful effects that riding through water can have on your bearings (if they are not sealed) and exposed moving parts—plan on lubricating your chain, derailleurs, inner wires, and so on, when you return home. Finally, regarding snow and ice, as much as possible just stay away from ice. Snow riding can be fun but if its deep, it can be very laborious. Maintaining momentum and avoiding buried obstacles are the two major tasks for snow riders. Also, the difficulty of steep ascents and descents are significantly magnified by a few inches of snow—most mountain bikers riding on snow prefer flat or nearly flat terrain.

APPENDIX D

Tools to Carry with You
As Angel Rodriguez tells the story . . .

One day I went down and got an ice cream cone (pecan-praline), and as I walked past the bus stop towards my bike, my friend Amy got off the bus. If you knew Amy you would have to stop and talk, especially if you saw her get off a bus. Amy rides her bike everywhere. I asked her what she was doing on the bus, and she proceeded to tell me about her theory of bike repair. It's a very simple theory: carry bus money and a bike lock. When your bike breaks down, lock it to something sturdy, take the bus home, get your car, go back to pick up the bike, and drop it off at your favorite bike shop. I was impressed. Not a spot of grease on her. Then I told her about my friend Herman.

When I first started cycling, Herman took us out on rides. Herman must have been forty or fifty at the time; hard for me to tell 'cause he still looks the same 14 years later. One day we were out riding, and my rear derailleur wasn't quite adjusted. And as it must always happen, I shifted into the spokes, tearing up my derailleur and breaking a few spokes - on the freewheel side, of course. I was ready to call Mom to come get me when Herman rolled up; he always seemed to be there when you needed him. He looked at the bike, said no problem, and unrolled his tool kit. Lo and behold, he had an extra rear derailleur, a few spokes of various lengths, a freewheel tool for every bike you could think of, plus a five-pound wrench to use on the freewheel tools. What a guy!

My conversation with Amy made me think about tool kits. Cyclists want to know, "What tools should I buy and when should I carry them?" There are two basic philosophies. One extreme says that you should maintain your bike well enough that you don't need to carry tools at all. Repair it at home, not on the road. These folks just carry phone money and have Mom come get them if something really goes wrong. The other extreme carries every possible tool to fix every possible problem on every possible bike.

My rule of thumb is that you should carry the tools to get you home from any distance you are not willing to walk.

What Ten Different Types of Cyclists Carry With Them
(Adding the items as you go.)

Amy	type 1	bus money and a lock
Minimalist	type 2	patch kit, tire levers, and pump
Smart Minimalist	type 3	spare tube
Smart Cyclist	type 4	basic tool kit:
		tiny vise grips (5 inch)
		pocket pro "T" wrench
		3,4,5,6 mm allens
		slot and Philips screw drivers
		8,9,10 mm sockets
		spoke wrench
		chain tool
Experienced	type 5	spare nuts, bolts and selected bearings
Touring Cyclist	type 6	spare spoke, freewheel tool, pocket vise
Smart Tourist	type 7	crankpuller, spare tire, chain lube
Traveling Tourist	type 8	pedal wrench
Good Samaritan	type 9	6, 7, and 8 above, for other kinds of bikes
Herman	type 10	big adjustable wrenches, bailing wire, and spare chain and freewheel and a rag to wipe your hands.

(Reprinted from *Seattle Bicycle Atlas* with permission of Carla Black and Angel Rodriguez.)

Editor's Note:
A word to the wise. There are no buses in the backcountry and telephones are few and far apart. You need to be your own Herman in remote situations.

Angel Rodriguez produces a series of high-tech bike tools under the trade name Pocket Pro®

TOPO MAPS & GUIDEBOOKS FROM FINE EDGE PRODUCTIONS

MOUNTAIN BIKING AND RECREATION TOPO MAPS

Santa Monica Mountains, ISBN 0-938665-23-5	$9.95
Eastern High Sierra–Mammoth, June, Mono, ISBN 0-938665-21-9	$9.95
San Bernardino Mountains, ISBN 0-938665-32-4	$9.95
San Gabriel Mountains – West, ISBN 0-938665-13-8	$8.95
North Lake Tahoe Basin, ISBN 1-879866-06-4	$8.95
South Lake Tahoe Basin, ISBN 1-879866-07-2	$8.95

GUIDE BOOKS
Mountain Biking the High Sierra

Guide 1, Owens Valley and Inyo County, Second Edition, ISBN 0-938665-01-4	$9.95
Guide 2, Mammoth Lakes and Mono County, Third Edition, ISBN 0-938665-15-4	$9.95
Guide 3A, Lake Tahoe South, Third Edition, ISBN 0-938665-27-8	$10.95
Guide 3B, Lake Tahoe North, Second Edition, ISBN 0-938665-07-3	$9.95
Guide 13, Reno/Carson City, ISBN 0-938665-22-7	$10.95

Mountain Biking the Coast Range

Guide 4, Ventura County and the Sespe, Third Edition, ISBN 0-938665-18-9	$9.95
Guide 5, Santa Barbara County, Third Edition, ISBN 0-938665-04-9	$9.95
Guide 7, Santa Monica Mountains, Second Edition, ISBN 0-938665-10-3	$9.95
Guide 8, Saugus District, Angeles N.F. with Mt. Pinos, ISBN 0-938665-09-8	$9.95
Guide 9, San Gabriel Mountains, Angeles N.F., ISBN 0-938665-11-1	$9.95
Guide 10, San Bernardino Mountains, ISBN 0-938665-16-2	$10.95
Guide 11, Orange County and Cleveland National Forest, ISBN 0-938665-17-0	$9.95
Guide 12, Riverside County & Coachella Valley, ISBN 0-938665-24-3	$10.95

Other books available:

Mountain Biking Northern California's Best 100 Trails, ISBN 0-938665-31-6	$14.95
Mountain Biking Southern California's Best 100 Trails, ISBN 0-938665-20-0	$14.95
Favorite Pedal Tours of Northern California, ISBN 0-938665-12-X	$12.95
What Shall We Do Tomorrow–Mammoth Lakes Sierra, ISBN 0-938665-30-8	$10.95
What Shall We Do Tomorrow–North Lake Tahoe/Truckee, ISBN 0-9633056-0-3	$8.95
What Shall We Do Tomorrow–South Lake Tahoe/Carson Pass, ISBN 0-9633056-1-1	$10.95
Ski Touring the Eastern High Sierra, ISBN 0-938665-08-1	$8.95
Exploring California's Channel Islands, an Artist's View, ISBN 0-938665-00-6	$6.95

Additional books and maps in process; manuscripts are solicited.
For current titles and prices, please send SASE.
To order any of these items, see you local dealer or order direct. Please include $2.50 for shipping. California residents add sales tax. 20% discount on orders of 5 or more items.

Fine Edge Productions, Route 2, Box 303, Bishop, California 93514